The Alpha's Mate: A Tale of Romance and Werewolves

TINA ROFFE

Table of Contents

Summary

As far as Leah is aware, she is a human. Leah's mother left the family when she was eight years old, but the girl has since learned that her mother is a werewolf who has met her partner. With the death of her father in a vehicle accident, the one constant in her life was gone. In the pack grounds, Leah must now reside with her mother. It comes as a shock to Alpha Carson that his mate might be the only human he has allowed to remain. Leah has some trouble adapting to the new restrictions, but her true problems arise when she finds out the truth about his parents and her origins.

Prologue

With rage rising in me, I glanced out the window.

My irritation with her increased as my father spoke more and more about her.

He turned his attention back to the road and continued, "She wants to see us, Leah." She desired... Before he could continue, I interrupted him. To which I said, "She left us when I was just eight," facing him. She never called or texted me; I guess she didn't want me. I don't know why I should approach her now.

Everything inside of me was driven by anger.

To her disgrace, she abandoned me.

The old man he was sighed.

After football practice, we were on our way home. I scored the game-winning goal for us. My dad suggested a party, but then he said he needed to have a serious conversation first. I complied since he seemed to be sick, but I had no idea it was going to involve my mother's abandonment.

To my surprise, my dad said nothing in response to my query.

My mother is the subject of this conversation. From the time I was a baby until I was eight years old, my mom was there, and then she disappeared. As she was out with who knows who, my dad and I remained at home.

My dad and I both avoided talking about her. Just the two of us who were OK with us. We worked well together. Even on Sundays, my dad and I would do something wild with my kid. Sure, we did things like eating chocolate for the morning or taking part in a zip line adventure, but I enjoyed every minute of it.

A few things began to catch my attention. My father kept bringing up my mother at supper, and things had been off for a few days. I was taken aback since we hadn't brought up her name in years.

He was first devastated by her departure. Most evenings, I could hear him sobbing himself to sleep; he eventually got over her, yet he never remarried. I won't say he never had a girlfriend because he had one, and some of them were very nice, yet he never felt compelled to settle down with anybody. My mom was probably to fault for it.

I encouraged him to start dating again, yet he never confirmed or denied my suggestion. When I found out he was out on dates, I pretended not to notice when I found two empty bottles in the sink the next morning. The only lady he's ever desired is me, he said. I know it's sad, but that's just my Dad.

My father interrupted my thoughts with, "Leah, she only wants to see you."

I gave him a murderous look.
Shouting, "I am blind to the lady who left me for nine years," was my response. I never received a birthday or holiday card from her, and she never contacted me. "What type of lady would do that?"

My dad had turned around and I glanced at him.

He finally exclaimed, "That's enough, Leah." The talk is over; "You will be seeing her next week."

For a long while, I just looked at him. Did you take him at his joke? The decision seemed to be up to me. I was quite furious. I let out a "like hell" yell. You can't make me see the lady if I don't want to, and I have no intention of doing so.

When I gave him the evil eye, his attention wandered back to me. He started to say "Please," but was interrupted by honking.

During a moment of confusion, my dad jerked his head back and swerved to avoid a collision. He refocused his attention on the road ahead of us and straightened us up.

The adrenaline was flowing through my veins; that was a near call.

My dad was silent for a while, but then he started talking again. He assured her, "Leah, your mom, will explain everything." I can't help you, so go ahead and chat with her.

I just looked straight ahead, ignoring him.

The home was where I felt most comfortable.

The lady infuriated me.

I don't remember when I first began to dislike her, but it was probably when she started showing up at every school event, concert, or anything my friends were involved in. Several times I waited for my mother to arrive, but she never did.

I suppose I stopped hoping she'd return to me.

I beg you, Leah," he pleaded. Do it for me, please. There was a moment when I had to shut my eyes. That isn't exactly my favorite phrase. When she got a personal call, she would always say that. When she needed to take her medication, she told me to "go in there" Shhh, don't tell Dad. Have you got the ability to help me with that?

I had to tell my father a fib about a phone conversation since my mother forced me to. Who would do that to a child of seven?

I peeled open my eyelids and looked forward through the window.

'Leah?' he yelled after her.

I turned to him and murmured, "I wish I had never said it." Asking, "Can you do that for me?" Pops? I'd rather eat junk and have a hot poker stuck in my eye than have to deal with her again.

Leah, he snarled between gritted teeth.

I gave him a puzzled look.

For the life of me, I couldn't figure out why he was being so cruel to me. I didn't want to make contact with her, especially after all this time since she wasn't a mother then.

I opened my mouth to speak when suddenly the rear of the vehicle was struck by something, sending us careening forward.

I let out a loud yell.

Following then, everything moved quickly and furiously.

Someone had walked right into our backs. The automobile backed up but then slammed into us again.

I yelled, "Dad," as I clutched the door knob.

My dad didn't say anything in response.

When we slammed into the automobile in front of us, I peered around through the windshield.
I was wearing my seatbelt, yet I had it slack because I didn't like the way it felt when it was too tight, and I shot forward, hitting my skull on the dashboard.

To clear my vision, I shut my eyes and raised my head. As I glanced over, I saw that my father was unresponsive.

I yelled, "DAD!" as I frantically tried to reach him, but dazzling lights blocked my path. My head snapped back and I slammed against the door, knocking me fully unconscious and plunging me into the darkness I screamed as whatever it was came right at us, striking my father's side with a tremendous bang.

Chapter 1

All around me were beeping sounds.

I was lost.

I was unable to open my eyes, yet I felt comfortable.

A few people whispered to one another. I made a few attempts to talk and move, but my head hurt too much and all I could do was grunt.

The name "Leah" is whispered. How about you?

The light was overwhelming when I opened my eyes slowly.

This makes me moan.

A lady inside a white coat finally came into focus after I blinked many times.

It was returned by her in the form of a grin.

"Leah," she said. Doctor Nadia here. You had a car crash. What occurred, do you know?

I tried to shake it off, but my head was already hurting.

I scratched my head and mumbled, "Oh," attempting to figure out what was on top of my head.

A little later, I cast my gaze toward Doctor Nadia. There was a sigh from her. You have a severe concussion, honey, she warned. "Stop moving about."

Everything she stated, I did.

My eyes landed on her.

Nadia, the doctor, smiled again.

Where was Dad when I needed him?

"I can't find my dad." I looked at her in awe and inquired.

A look of surprise crossed Doctor Nadia's face, but she said nothing. Her eyes darted to the side, where I was standing. I turned to see what had caught her attention and was taken aback by the sight of the person standing there.

My mother.

I don't even know why she's here.

I couldn't look at her without becoming queasy.

Who took my Dad?
The environment was full of beeping sounds.

Honestly, I had no idea where I was.

Even though I couldn't see where I was lying, I knew it was a comfortable surface.

There were some low whispers in the background. I moaned as the agony raced through my brain and I attempted to talk and move.

In a low voice, "Leah," is said. "Are you awake?"

I opened my eyes cautiously, but the light was too intense.

I have to sigh.

After many unsuccessful efforts, I blinked aside the haze and peered at a lady inside a white coat.

As he smiled, she returned the gesture.

Leah, she called out. It's me, Dr. Nadia. You were involved in a collision. Do you have any idea what went down?"

The more I moved my head, the more my head hurt.

I scratched my head and mumbled, "Oh," as I tried to identify the object perched there.

After a little pause, I met Doctor Nadia's gaze. Sighing, she looked about. "You have a major concussion, dear," she reassured me. "Stop what you're doing right now."

That's what she wanted, so I complied.

Took a peek at her.

The doctor's grin returned.

I was all alone; where had Dad gone?

Where is my Dad? When I stared at her, I asked.

Doctor Nadia's expression shifted, but she remained silent. She cast a swift look to my side.

As I looked in the direction she was pointing, I was taken aback to realize who it was.

My mother.

But why the heck was she even here?

Feeling queasy, I continued to gaze at her.

Daddy, where were you?
A few mutters emanated out of each, but I paid them no mind. I just wanted some quiet time to myself. I had to mourn the loss of the one constant in my life.

I avoided eye contact with each of them. Dr. Nadia and my mother had already departed since I heard the door wide open and shut.

I burst into tears shortly after the door closed.

Extreme sobbing was mine.

As I shut my eyes, I found myself at the scene of the vehicle crash. As though watching a flashback movie, memories flooded back.

I just realized that my dad and I were in a vehicle accident.

I don't recall exactly how many vehicles collided with ours, but it seemed like they came at us from every direction.

The fight we had was over with my mom, and I'll never forget it. She had no business being at a medical facility. I avoided her like the plague.

I couldn't imagine spending time with her.

After sobbing for a whole hour, I finally got some shut-eye.

A dream came to me so strongly that it was eerily reminiscent of a horror film, and I didn't stay asleep for long. Even though I usually prefer horror films, I found this one to be somewhat tedious. The crash was mentioned, albeit in an inaccurate way. Someone was in the center of the road, and I was riding a shotgun. In an attempt to escape him, my dad swerved and collided with an oncoming vehicle. When other cars slammed into us, the guy moved toward ours. This individual approached me and unlocked the door.

When I could take no more, I yelled and sprang out of bed. The guy had an odd odor, like stale eggs. That gave me the need to vomit.

I felt like I was about to collapse from the heat and exertion.

"That was simply a dream," a voice remarked from my side as it drew close.
My palm went to my chest as I let out my fear, yet I still turned to see the source of the voice.

She was the subject of my intense concentration.

And now she was back.

My mother.

Why might they leave me alone? This is what I had in mind.

"Hello," she greeted me.

For a while, I was silent.

"Leah, I…" she continued, but I shuddered, which was a poor idea. I forgot everything Doctor Nadia said to me & all about the pain.

When my head began to pound, I shut my eyes.

Fuck.

A question: "Why are you even here?" I questioned her through gritted teeth as the pain receded. "I don't want you around here."

My mother glanced at me. She seemed shocked by what I had to say. She reassured Leah, "I'm here to care for you." Since your father is no longer there to correct me, I assume he has informed you about our meeting. I interrupted her mid-sentence. "What, you planned to storm the castle and seize power?" As the rage swept over me again, I yelled.

It wasn't going to happen, either.

'I'm not coming with you,' I yelled. During the last eight years, you've made no effort to get in touch with me. To assume that I desire you to be part of my life at this time is naive.

My mom seemed upset, but I didn't take it personally.

"I'm living with Lucy," I said. I'm safe in her mother's care. There's still a month of school remaining, and I'm not skipping out on it to hang out with you.

My mom constantly shifts her weight from foot to foot. "Leah, users my daughter," mom said.

I said, "GET THE FUCK OUT."
She was staring at me, immobile. I didn't feel bad that my mother was offended by my words. I don't know what she expected would occur. I'd just throw myself into her arms. If I were still seven years old when Mom departed, I probably would have thought about her more often than I have in the last year or even the past three years.

I yelled at her, "GET THE HELL OUT," which caught her off guard. "Stay far away from me," she said.

The door opened, and in strolled Lucy and her mom, Dani, while my mom scooted closer to the bed.

My mother paused to look.

Dani sent a compassionate glance my way but then moved to my mom. Do you agree with me that "enough is enough?" She spoke it while staring mutely.

I was afraid to breathe normally.

Dani was just as familiar with my mom as she was with my dad since they had grown friends over the years. My father has been getting some support from her me. Dani had emotions for him, but she never showed them; he never saw her as more than a friend.

As my mother saw Dani, she clenched her hands and gave her an intense look.

Lucy, my closest friend, walked up from behind Dani and I saw her. While I watched our mums continue to stare at one another, Lucy walked up and took my hand.

My mother gave a dejected sigh as she turned to me. She sighed, "Alright," and left the room.

As soon as she was out of sight, I let out a deep sigh.

Dani approached me, beaming. "Are you all right, honey?" she inquired.

I averted my eyes from her and hoped the door would stay closed.

My eyes landed on Dani. I brought my knees to my breast and muttered, "I'm alright," but the tears had started again and my sadness had returned.

In my mind, a picture of my dad sprang up.

I needed him (my Dad) more than ever. I needed him here, but he wasn't anymore.

I don't know how the heck I'd get by without him.

Chapter 2

My daughter's bedroom door held my attention.

I've never in my life been so anxious and afraid. I last saw her quite some time ago.

I heard a howl from my wolf. She missed her dog, but I understood how she felt; it was quite evident that she despised me after I met her dad a few days before.

She whimpered, "I want a pup," but I could relate to her sentiments and could only sigh. I anticipated difficulty, but this was horrible.

My companion was interested in joining us, but I felt it was important for Leah and me to have a conversation first. She has no idea who he is or anything about our world.

When I let my mind wander, it revisited every choice I'd made that had led me to this point.

I finally got in touch with her dad after eight years and asked to see our daughter. I asked Ryan to meet with me despite his initial resistance. As we started chatting, I knew it was too late to do anything about it.

At college, I was in love with a person named Larry. Being the lone werewolf at the time, I left my pack to attend this university. I was the first person in my family to attend college, and one of the few members of my tribe to do so.

My parents were and were very pleased. Everything changed when I met Larry at a party.

That was wrong, and I knew it since he wasn't my mate. Back in the day, Larry was what you could have called a geek. Yet he was naive and charming in a way I had never seen before, at least not among the men in our pack.

I developed a fascination with Larry throughout our time together as a college couple. I had to break the news to my parents after I graduated from college; they weren't exactly happy, but they eventually warmed up to him. My mom and dad came to see us and they both adored him. Once my parents went for the weekend, I informed him of our kind as they had instructed. After a lot of probing, Larry eventually came to terms with the news.

A home was purchased and we both found teaching positions at the local elementary school within a few months. I became pregnant with Leah two years later when everything was beautiful.

My life finally felt whole.
My wolf never once brought up the subject of my mate; she was happy with Larry and adored him just as much as I do.

During the first five years, my family and I thought we were the luckiest people alive. The word that my father had been assaulted and badly wounded came just after Leah turned five. My mother was in a state and asked that I return home. My mother informed me that outsiders had invaded the pack and murdered its alpha and other leaders.

Mother urged me to return home to assist care for Dad. Unfortunately, I had to leave Larry and Rachel behind while I stayed for a few weeks. Before I ever started seeing Larry, my parents knew about me and Larry. I was too afraid of what they might say, so I told Larry that they were familiar with her. I committed the cardinal sin of having a human kid outside of marriage.

We could leave Leah with our buddy, and Larry volunteered to accompany along. I told him he shouldn't be there since it would be too gruesome for him. I, too, was concerned about his well-being.

This was the first occasion I had ever left Leah alone, and I panicked.

I departed that evening. When I pulled away from the curb, I glanced back to see my husband clutching our baby daughter's hand. I was completely shattered by that.

When I first joined the pack, I took care of my father with the other members. My mother made a huge deal out of nothing, and my dad was OK, but I wanted to make sure he was alright, so I remained for a long. Rogue wolves assaulting our pack was something I hadn't heard of in a very long time. We were a powerful gang, but many things had altered during my absence. The day my mate and his pack arrived to pay their respect to the alpha was the day I had intended to depart for good.

The wolf inside me was content, then life hit me like a storm. I was taken aback. I had given all hope of ever finding him, and things were in shambles anyhow. He needed to know about my family and my experiences living among people.

I didn't know what to do and it shattered my heart.

My friend made a huge deal out of the fact that we are friends. Others around me were ecstatic, but I couldn't show it. During our conversation, I found out that my companion was a fierce fighter. A few hours later, he went, but not before promising to stick around with the wolf pack so he could be with me.

I appreciated the compliment but said nothing. I didn't say goodbye to my pack mates or my family that night.

I got in my car and headed back to my family. I had to spend time with my kids, but it was before everything changed.

At first, my wolf reacted negatively whenever Larry was around or made any attempt to approach me or the pack. After coming home for two weeks, I was on edge all the time, and conflicts between Larry and me often broke out.

During a particularly nasty argument, I casually told Larry that I had finally found the one. He was aware of werewolves and their need for a mate, but I convinced him that my wolf had other plans. When he inquired as to my desires, I was at a loss for words. When I did it, I saw Larry's heart break in two.

One night, he up and departed with Leah.
My folks had been on the phone constantly pleading with me to return home. They said that, like the moon goddess, I should abandon Larry in favor of my true love.

My wolf longed to be reunited with her mate after Larry abducted her the night before. Our dog was completely overlooked. She completely ignored Leah in favor of our other half.

I sobbed and worried about them at home. Larry and Leah returned the next day. I planned on taking a break from making any decisions for a day or two. But it didn't last long since my partner arrived there and insisted I return home with him.

Larry and Leah were working together while Larry was away. Our relationship was tense in every way. My friend Larry had no idea I was hiding out here.

I promised my friend I'd go with them, but I had a career here and wanted to take care of some business first.

So, I had myself in a jam. My only thought was for my six-year-old daughter, Leah; I hated the idea of abandoning her, but it seemed I had no choice.

When I had to quit my work a year early, I recall stepping in and explaining the situation. I had to close out the year or face financial penalties and legal repercussions.

In the end, I opted to return with my partner, but I informed him I had to complete my year at work since I was glad to have a year to figure out exactly what I would do. To be closer to me, he accepted and began a job teaching other packs in the area.

For a whole year, I was living a double life. I'd spend a couple of nights with my partner and the rest of the time with my family.

By the end of the year, Larry had become emotionally distant. Knowing that my partner would eventually find out, I stopped having sexual relations with him. I had it all figured out, until one day Larry walked up to me standing in front of his partner, and handed me some papers to sign.

That astonished and angered my friend. Honestly, I had no clue what was going on. After following me and seeing me with him, Larry reported this to me. He was aware of the situation. Larry pounced on me and demanded that I sign the papers.

Never before had I seen him so enraged, yet I could also see the pain in his eyes.

As I went over the paperwork, I saw that Larry was granted complete custody of Leah.
Even though it shattered my heart, I knew I had to do it.

Once I had signed everything, Larry had already taken the papers with him.

I remained with my partner and had to fill him in on what had happened, but I left out Leah since that wasn't relevant. Without me, she'd be much happier.

It was on that day that I decided to go.

I always suspected Leah was a wolf, yet she never displayed any of the classic symptoms when she was a kid.

A loud crash from the hall jolted me out of my reminiscences. As if to clear my mind, I shook my head.

Since I wasn't there, I understood why Leah despised me. I lacked the courage to speak out about her or keep quiet about it.

I made a bold move a few weeks earlier when I decided to contact Larry. Being sick, I had traveled quite a distance. My desire to communicate with Leah was sincere.

When We left, I was very much focused on my partner. I had another pair of puppies after we coupled and marked one another for two weeks. Even though it was Leah's birthday, I couldn't help but think about her. When one of the kids did something, I pondered whether or if Leah enjoyed doing the same things.

My parents reassured me that I had made the correct decision when I finally joined the pack. Because I never filled them in on Leah, I knew they had no idea. To tell them I had a kid with a guy who wasn't my partner would have been too humiliating. My mom and dad were law-abiding citizens who instilled that value in my brother, Julian, and me.

A disgusting person, that was me.
The ringing of my phone startled me out of my reverie. The item was taken from my pocket.

Hey, Josh.

After giving it a quick swipe to answer, I brought the phone up to my ear. What's up, sweetie? Asking, "How is she?"

I stopped thinking. he along with my other children were all I could think of.

After being assaulted by rogues, the pack finally drove me insane after a few years. It was like being thrust back into the same situation I was in when my mother was hurt. There were times when I speculated that maybe I could have stayed with Larry as well as Leah if I hadn't returned to the pack. I was taken to the hospital and told not to contact anybody, including Josh.

While I was in the hospital for a few days while everybody was trying to uncover what was wrong with me, I remember finally getting some alone time with Josh and spilling the beans about Leah.

He just looked at me, didn't say a word, and eventually left me alone just to process the news that I was carrying another man's kid.

The tears lasted for hours.

When he returned, he probed for details.

When I closed my eyes to block off the painful recollection, he murmured, "Love, you still there?" My wolf looked back at me, her eyes filled with pain.

She despises me, I thought to myself as I popped my eyes open and faced the entrance. Her dad has passed on, and she despises me.

Hunny, he greeted her. She just needs some quiet time to whine, Dad. Will Leah be coming back with you?

I was still shaken by the previous ranting, so I kept my mouth shut. She favors hanging out with her pal over hanging out with me. Just "I don't know," I said. There are just three weeks left of school for her, so I may hold off until then. I may have to engage in social services.

He questioned, "Why?" Because you're her mother, she belongs with you.

I said, "I know." I cut off all communication with her when I left. I wasn't her mother at all. All my rights are being waived.

Josh stayed silent.

I still have every piece of paper that Larry sent me; I provided him my address and he sent me nothing but paperwork, not even pictures of Leah. The whole custody agreement I signed kept popping up in my mind. While recuperating in the hospital, I gave Josh explicit directions on where to locate everything. I recall his bringing those to me, but I displayed the paperwork for his inspection.
How I was behaving over him and the reason for my being so cold toward the kids suddenly made perfect sense to him.

I told my parents, who hadn't talked to me in a long time. That I had hidden their granddaughter away caused them so much embarrassment and sorrow.

Josh spat, "Have Julian come to you." He is the top dog in his field. We can put up a fight and force her to move in with us.

Josh's willingness to welcome Leah into the family was much appreciated by me. She was human, but I wasn't. I felt responsible to protect her.

Alright, I gave in.

The lady who had been gazing about when the door to Leah's room opened finally settled on me.

My inner wolf wanted to tear the woman's head off due to the way she talked to us, but I had to keep her in check.

She gave me a blank look but came over nonetheless. It's time for you to go, she told him. You have no business identifying as her. Where have you been hiding out for so long?

No response was required from my end.

That's none of your business," I mumbled.

As the phone was still up to my ear, I assumed Josh is now on the other end. A deep growl got through to me.

I don't care what you're trying to say about Leah, she said. "Get out of here! She doesn't want you!"

She was the subject of my intense concentration. I agreed with her assessment, but as Leah's father, I had to be there for her.

I clamped my jaw tight. Quite fine, I mused. I'm leaving, but we're not out of the woods yet.

I swiveled around and left the room. As I walked away, I could see that she was following me.

She hissed, "I will murder that human," but I paid little attention to my wolf's threats.

"Hunny," Josh said. How are you feeling?

I felt furious and heartbroken at the same time.

I suddenly had a flash of sadness because of how much I missed Larry. What I missed most was just talking to you. It was Josh who recommended I speak with Larry. He lied to Leah about being on business and met us midway.
Larry informed me that he was no longer interested in me. Despite his deceit, I was relieved that he had acknowledged my existence.

They discussed the situation with Leah, and he and Josh came to a decision.

Are you there, honey? This is what Josh said.

I abruptly halted and rounded the bend.

My mind became determined, and I resolved to defend Leah no matter how much she loathed me.

I called out for Julian, telling him to meet me. I'll need his assistance soon.

Well, he finally conceded.

While I was leaving the hospital, we continued our conversation.

After a few glances around, I made my way to the forest's edge. As no one on Earth had heard of our race, I had to tread carefully.

My wolf had to get away, but I had to tread lightly.

The hotel owner was a wolf, so I went back there. He didn't expect to see me, but when he heard that Larry and Leah had been in a vehicle accident in which Larry had perished, I realized I had to come & fetch her.

I felt like I owed it to Leah to go to bat for her.

Chapter 3

I asked Doctor Nadia whether Lucy could remain with me after she and Dani went after visiting hours were finished. I remained up while she slept.

As a result, I was unable to rest. Every time I rested my head, I was overcome with a sense of being trapped. When Lucy awoke, I lied and said I'd been asleep the whole time.

I was relieved that I didn't see my mother again that night.

In the morning, Dani returned. After a full day of visiting, Lucy and Dani finally had to go.

I needed to sleep badly, but I couldn't get any.

Before returning home, Dr. Nadia remained with me to make sure I was comfortable.

I feigned to sleep through her departure and the arrival of the nurses, but as quickly as they had departed, I was wide awake.

I couldn't get to sleep because every time I did, my dad would be staring at me.

The idea of him brought tears to my eyes.

When I was a kid, all I wanted was my dad back.

Dani said she would assist me with the funeral of my dad. In return for her kindness, I urged her to act as she believed was appropriate and take charge of the situation.

My dad was indeed a decent guy who had some nice acquaintances. I expected a tiny turnout for the burial, but Doctor Nadia said I wouldn't be able to leave the hospital for many more days.
Leaving the hospital gave me the willies, so I'm glad I'm stuck here for the time being. I was completely at a loss for what to do next. I hadn't made any plans regarding where to go, but I realized I wouldn't be traveling anyplace with my parents. The lady wasn't even someone I knew.

Since Dani had thrown her out the morning I woke up, I hadn't seen her.

Thankfully, there wasn't much noise at the hospital. I wanted to get some shut-eye, but nothing I tried worked.

As I turned to look at the door after sensing motion, I saw a shadow and realized someone was peering inside.

I heard a knock on the door, but I couldn't see who it was.

As the minutes passed without hearing who was calling, I sat back on the bed. I rolled over so my back was to the door and I could stare at the wall.

There was no way I was going to be able to sleep soon.

Insomnia appeared to be on my side, but I knew that Doctor Nadia wouldn't let me go until she was satisfied that I was well. No matter how many times I assured her I was OK, she had to know I wasn't. My head ached because of the lack of sleep.

I was startled out of my reverie by the sound of the door opening, and I quickly closed my eyes so as not to alert anybody to my presence. Two distinct sets of footfalls led me to believe that someone had entered the space.

I thought I detected some shifting, but nobody said out.

What's her status? whispered a man's voice I didn't recognize.

Doctor Nadia said she's doing much better, the woman's voice, who I recognized at once, said.

I don't even know why she's here.

My veins were boiling with rage. She was aware that I did not want her to be present.

When I sat up and looked back, I saw two shocked expressions staring back at me. Astonished: "Why the heck are you here?" I inquired.

My mom turned to look at me, however the guy next to her tilted his head. He began, "I wanted to..." but I thought about it and turned back to stare at my mother. "I told you to leave us alone and go away yesterday."

Her name was Leah, but I rolled my eyes at her. When I glanced at her, my throbbing head pain suddenly returned. I raised my hand and held it above my head.
The sound of her hand reaching up to me made me glance up and see my mother. I sent the lady a

retaliatory glance. I shouted at her, "Get the fuck away from me," and distanced myself from her.

I shot a brief peek at the guy who was studying me intently. "Where do your eyes take you?" I made a sneering face and put my palm to my head.

There was a grin on the man's face. He caught me off guard when he stated, "You behave precisely like your mom did when you were a youngster."

I looked at him for a while, but my irritation with him and my mother eventually took over and I became angry again.

I just said, "I don't care." Between the two of them, I cast my gaze. They had the same facial characteristics, including blue eyes and mousy brown hair.

The guy approached closer, setting down a sheet of paper. I tried to focus my eyes on it, but the room was too dim for me to see what it was. What is that? I questioned with a grimace as I looked back at him.

There was a grin on the man's face. Well, sweetie," he continued, looking at my mom and then back to me. "There's a paper saying you and your pals will graduate high school next month and go home to mother."

"WHAT?" I let out a loud shout. Not going to happen.

I didn't give a damn whether mum was upset.

Really, what did she think would happen? I was no longer the child left behind, the one who waited at the foot of the stairs for her mother to return. I was seventeen for crying out loud; surely I could manage without her.

She yanked me out of my reverie with an "I'm sorry, Leah" statement. My mother moved closer to me. You must stay with a relative until you are of legal age to live on your own.

I snarked back at her, "Oh, that's not you," and backed away from her.

The muscles in my mom's face tightened.

A throat was cleansed. It's enough, he said. You can't talk to your mother that way. You and she are officially moving in with one another at the month's end.

I faced the guy and scowled at him.

I said, "Nah." That's not going to happen.

Transfixed, I looked at them.

I stared at my mom and said, "You think you can control every aspect of my life once you're back, I've got one more thing coming." "I'm going to make your life very miserable."

She said, "You don't mean that."

I laughed out loud.

The correct response was, "Your kidding right," which I expressed by saying. It's been eight years since you abandoned me, so why don't you just let me live with my buddy and her parents for another year until I'm an adult?

My mother didn't say anything, but I could see I had upset her.

A voice could be heard, and the guy said. He started to say, "You need to be..." but I interrupted him by shaking my head. You need me to be what?" Huh!" I said, giving him the evil eye. You would like me to stay with the lady who left my father and me, the one who has never asked after me, who has never followed my career, who has never seen any of my performances.

With tears flowing down my cheeks, I turned to gaze at them and my mother.
"I always waited at the foot of the stairs for you to return," I confessed.

My mother allowed herself to shed a single tear before closing her eyes. I said, "I blamed myself." I used to spend days there, but eventually, I accepted the fact that you weren't coming back.

My eyes landed on her.

I told him that he and my father would be happier without me. He never once mentioned you. I knew you had injured him. He was both my mother and father, therefore Dad made amends for it all.

I blinked my eyes and scowled at them while I rubbed the side of my head.

"Go out," I commanded. Once the month is over, it's alright with me if we have to part ways. But until then, I don't want you here. I can't wait to be picked up by you and not have to see you again. I'll be living with a friend and her mom at their house till then.

The guy started to say something, but my mum cut him off. My mom shook her head and drew his attention. My mother returned my gaze and nodded silently.

They were about to depart when an idea struck me.

My response was, "Well, I don't want you there for Dad's burial." On the day you went, you said your farewells.

My mother paused for a while without saying anything, then continued on her way out the door.

The door shut behind her, but the guy remained there and stared at me in surprise.

He said, "You are one cruel little one."

With a grimace on my face, I responded, "I'm not that small." You should probably pursue her, right?

The guy looked me dead in the eye but sighed. "At the month's conclusion, you'll meet your friend's home, and your mom to pick you up."

I just stepped away from him and didn't say a word.

As I heard that door close, I slipped even lower on the bed.

I rolled over onto my side and started crying.

I feel terrible for being a diva, but I don't know what else to do. I had to deal with my mother abandoning me years ago and then losing my father.

I moaned in pain as my head pounded.

The agony was too much for me to bear.

I clicked the nurse call button and she arrived very immediately.

Who knows, maybe she allowed my mother and that guy in.

The nurse prescribed me some powerful medications.
I expected to be sent to sleep, and if a nightmare was waiting for me when I shut my eyes, I pray it didn't come.

My eyelids were heavy after a while, and I soon found myself fast asleep.

Even as darkness engulfed me, the same image resurfaced in my head.

The recurring dream continued.

My eyelids sprung up and I puffed desperately to get a breath of air.

Despite the lack of light, I managed to remain alert.

Either this pain or my lack of sleep was going to end me, and I clutched my palm to my head in agony.

Chapter 4

My mom and that guy showed up at the hospital that night, and it's been 2 days since then.

Today, I was supposed to leave the hospital alongside Dani and Lucy and spend the night with them. As Dani read the note that had been left for her, she was taken aback. She explained to me that because a judge had signed the letter, there was not nothing she had to do.

All day long, I sobbed.

in addition, I just experienced the loss of my dad, but now I stood to lose but one folk I had ever called a friend as well.

I'm going to be moving in there with your mother at the finish of the month. The fact that she had a home was unknown to me. Even though Dani attempted to inform me, I was uninterested.

My thoughts drifted and I devised a strategy without consulting my mother, and I was determined. When I reached eighteen, I was released from juvenile detention.

I plan to relocate far away from my mother.

As Doctor Nadia delivered my pills to Dani, I sat on our bed. To prepare for my departure after the month, she instructed me on what to do and insisted on seeing me beforehand.

While we were leaving the hospital, I kept my mouth shut.

In a haze, I made my way out of the hospital and to my vehicle.

Lucy and I rode together in the backseat, where she was quite calm. She was aware of my mental state but respected my desire for privacy as I sorted things out. As Dani drove out of the hospital's premises, I gazed out the window.

The closest hospital to our home was a twenty-minute drive.

My pulse quickened as Dani turned into the street. Dani and Lucy were my neighbors to the west, although they were three homes away. When Dani drove past the home and into her driveway, I closed my eyes.

When the vehicle finally stopped, I yanked the door open and hopped out. As I reoriented myself, I saw my home in the distance.

The home I spent my whole life in.

I would go across, but I just couldn't do it. We were late leaving that morning, and I remembered seeing the breakfast dishes in the washbasin as we hurried out the door. My father picked me up and told me he had something important to discuss with me. That was after I finished football practice.

Lucy, who was standing next to me, said, "Are you okay?" I kept my eyes fixed on the home at all times. Weakly, "yes," I replied. "I have to make a trip over there; I do need stuff."

I felt a tear roll down my cheek.

Suddenly, Lucy's hand was in mine. We can meet again whenever you're ready, she added.

I gave her a glance and a kind grin. Thank you, I remarked.

Dani sighingly strolled up behind us. You may visit the house the next day, she said Leah. "Let me go over and get something for you. Make a list, and after we've gotten you situated, I'll go grab it.

I glanced back and nodded at her.
I turned around now and followed Lucy inside the home as she held my arm.

Lucy ushered me up to my room as soon as I entered.

When we finally arrived, I took in my surroundings and stifled a chuckle. When Lucy and I were younger, we spent every weekend together, but we always slept in opposite beds.

Lucy's bed was made up of two blankets on each side and two pillows at either end.

"As we used to when we were kids," she said. A double bed and more space are welcome improvements.

After a moment, I nodded.

Lucy came over, helped lift me onto the bed's head, and climbed in with me. After settling down, I pulled the blanket up to my thighs.

My only serious wounds were to my forehead and a large, deep cut on my wrist.

I found out what occurred from Dani. My father was trapped, but rescuers broke their way in through my window to save me. Doctor Nadia appeared to assume that my palm had scraped across a glass shard when they dragged me through, but no one knows for sure how I acquired the cut.

It will take a few more days of covering it, yet it will heal eventually. There's a chance that I have a scar somewhere.

Oh my, now I have to think about the time I lost my Mom.

Lucy made a list to her mum of the things we were missing, having inquired what they were. I requested a variety of articles of clothing, pajamas, a brush, a toothbrush, a toothbrush, a phone, and a charger.

After receiving the list from Lucy, Dani departed. Before she went, though, Dani cooked for us. Lucy and I ate popcorn and watched a movie together. "Are you feeling all right?" When the movie began, Lucy questioned.

Indeed, I did say that.

Lucy was silent for a while before releasing a sigh. "I can't believe you'll only be staying with us for a month before returning home to your mother."

I just sat there and watched the TV, speechless, my thoughts racing.

Do you have a good understanding of her? she probed.

I shook my head and gave her the side eye. False, I responded. Eight years ago, she abandoned my father and me. There was zero communication between us.

Luca scowled. She questioned, "how did the physicians get a hold of her then?"

I gaped and thought back to my exchange with Dr. Nadia. They called her since my dad had her number saved in his phone and she was hiding out with Leah's parents.

The physicians found her number while going through my father's phone and called her to tell her what had occurred, as I said.

When I switched my attention back to the monitor, Lucy gazed at me. Whoa, she exclaimed.

After a moment, I nodded.

When we were kids, we loved seeing Willow, one of the best children's movies ever made.

Lucy got up when the movie was over and put on another one for us.

After waiting a while, Dani brought my belongings upstairs and set them on the floor before coming to get me. She extended her hand, and I received a picture frame as a gift. I just looked at it blankly. That was a photo of my dad and me.

Just a single tear trickled down my face.

He framed a recent picture of us and presented it for the first time a few weeks ago so I could display it with my other pictures on my dresser.

I offered Dani a feeble grin and raised an eyebrow. I mumbled, "thank you" as a sign of respect. There was a nod from her. That could assist you, so I brought one over here," she added.

Dani bent down and planted a kiss on my forehead. After glancing at Lucy, she returned her gaze to me. Don't stay out too late, she warned them. "You both need to get some rest; the ceremony is in 3 days."

After a moment, I nodded.

After a little pause, Lucy beamed. All right, mother," she finally conceded.

Dani gave me a grin as she stared at me. You don't want to take your mom with you, but she's the only family member still alive. I'm sorry, honey, but you just can't join us in this house.

Nothing came out of my mouth.

Oh, I have forgotten," she added as she was perched on top of both the bottom of his bed. The staff and children at Lucy's school were worried about you, she said. I've been informed by your professors that you didn't need to come in since you "completed all your tests and got results."

I took a startled glance at her.

Last week was my final test week. No one was supposed to return to class until everyone had received their results; then how could Dani get out about mine before everyone else?

My expression must have been telling when she responded to my query. Mr. Adams, who taught you, was good friends with your dad. If you weren't academically prepared for school, he was concerned about that. "You could just remain at home if you wanted to."

I was at a loss for words.

"You don't have to choose," Dani remarked to me with a little grin on her face.

Is it necessary for me to relocate in such a case? I began, but Dani interrupted me. No need to tell your mother. I won't be telling her. Please rest up and get well before seeing her, wherever she may be.

After a moment, I nodded.

I owe a huge debt of gratitude to Dani for that one. Likewise, I was exempt from attending classes. I was a normal high school student who made friends easily and went on a few dates with cute guys. The party atmosphere was not my cup of tea. Same with Lucy. We immediately hit it off and haven't been able to stay apart. As I left, I knew I would miss her.

I didn't need to attend classes. But in the meanwhile, what the heck was I supposed to do?

I relaxed back and saw that Lucy had selected "he Labrinth," a show comprised entirely of classic children's tales.

There was, however, one thing I was obligated to deal with, and I had no desire to. After a moment, I turned to Dani. "How should I proceed with our home?" A lump began to rise in my throat as I asked.

Lucy glanced up from the movie to exchange glances with her mom and me.

Mom just shrugged. The home may already be paid for, but I suppose we could look over everything just to be sure. If so, you could rent the apartment while you're still living at home with your mother, and then you'd have a place to go back to once you turn eighteen if you ever chose to leave her.

I looked at her blankly; it struck me as suspiciously as the beginnings of a plot.

Dani gazed at the TV while shaking her head. She assured him, "We will figure things out." I'm taking the next several days off, and we can sort things out after the burial.
After a moment, I nodded.

Dani gave me a peck on the forehead, then left the room.

I lowered my gaze to the picture frame I was clutching as Lucy and I returned to the movie.

The guy I had loved his entire life flashed before my eyes, and he was no longer there. How I long for his return.

A few drops hit the window of the frame.

I started weeping again.

Lucy took note but said nothing. She snuggled up to me while I wept quietly onto her shoulder throughout the movie.

Chapter 5

When she entered the home, I kept an eye on her from afar. I was invisible to her.

Keeping an eye on my kid made me feel like a stalker. Yet there was no way about it; I needed to check on her before I went.

Greenwich Pack is my pack as well as my home, and I was planning on returning there today. I needed to report the situation to my alpha.

Carson, the pack's Alpha, is three decades more mature than Leah. He became the pack leader when his father died.

Even as a youngster, Alpha Carson was able to assist his father and learn the ropes of the pack.

I groaned and turned around as the door closed.

Leah wasn't due to arrive for another month, so I had time to get my act together. I was nervous, but I knew I had to do it for the sake of myself and my friends Larry and Leah.

The hotel where our brother was going to wait for me was a short trek back, so I made my way there. He saw what I was up to but said nothing to me about it.

He was taken aback by Leah's behavior, yet she reminded him of himself with her short fuse.

It pained me when Leah talked to her about the things she did in the past, particularly waiting to see me come home, even though I knew I had harmed her.

I had to go back to my partner at home.

I had to break the news to Alec and Ethan, my oldest two kids, that their baby sister was due at the month's end.

My brother stared at me as I came closer to him. Has she returned?" he inquired.

After a moment, I nodded.

He let out a heavy sigh. He assured her that she would be OK.

We got in the vehicle together; the trip would take many hours, so we'd be there after sundown.

When my brother turned the key, I glanced across at him. Have Alpha Carson's minions gotten to you? I inquired.

I caught Julian's eye, and he nodded. We are all on our way back," he groaned. What have you chosen to do? he asks. When will she arrive?

I scowled. You know, I told him, you could just have told him that yourself. You wrote up the paperwork and got the real judge to sign it, right?

Julian cracked a grin.

I am aware of it, he said. But he needs to hear it from you in its entirety. Before you and Josh departed to come here, you filled him in on everything. He wasn't overjoyed to hear that you had a kid with a man, but he respected it.

I peered outside the glass. I didn't like it when others passed judgment on me, but ultimately, only Leah could do that. I'm sorry that I harmed her.
I reclined in my chair while Julian studied me intently. "Everything will work out," he assured me. Yet, "you have to explain our type to her."

My eyes were closed. To be told, I dread that section. As I tried to communicate with her, she immediately cut off all communication.

To hum along with the music, Julian turned on the radio. We left the little village I used to live in his car.

As Julian woke me up, I realized I'd been out for quite some time. I gave him the evil eye. "What?" That caused me to growl.

With a chuckle in his voice, he said, "We are here."

As I checked my surroundings, I saw that we had rejoined the herd. It was late and dark, yet the light in the alpha's office was still on.

This caused me to sigh.

Julian remarked, "He slept all drive here."

Without uttering a word, I got out of the vehicle. I didn't get much rest on the way to see Leah.

My wolf was sound sleeping; I could hear his soft snores in my mind. She was pacing back and forth until we came home and spotted Leah.

"Well, I suppose I needed it," I finally said. At that hotel, I didn't get a lot of shut-eye.

His head bobbed up and down.

His explanation? "I don't blame you."

I set out for the packed building and entered it. Julian accompanied me.

We arrived at Alpha Carson's workplace and knocked on the door.

He said, "Come in," and Julian let him inside.

Julian and I were the first ones inside.

Laughing, Alpha Carson raised her head. Jenny, you've returned, he greeted. "Julian."
Both of us bowed respectfully.

I glanced over to Alpha Carson as he sat at his desk-mounted computer.

Alpha Carson caught my gaze and chuckled. He complained, "The paperwork keeps piling up, and I've had to stop class also with warriors for the past three days."

After a moment, I nodded.

The door to his room opened, and in strolled his Beta and closest friend, Zain, just as I was about to unlock it. When he brushed by us and stopped next to Alpha Carson, he whispered, "Sorry."

I scowled.

Zain gave me a grin as he gazed at me. "I had to handle another situation at school," he stated.

Women were vying for the attention of both Alpha Carson and Beta Zain since neither had partners. Although Alpha Carson was preoccupied with the well-being of the pack, Beta Zain was preoccupied with finding a partner. I figured as much since I hadn't witnessed him with a lady in quite some time.

As Alpha Carson swallowed his clean throat, he snapped me out of my reverie. He finally addressed her, "Jenny, can you remind us how much you decided?"

I gave him a knowing look and nodded. Certainly, Alpha, I murmured, casting a glance at Julian, who nodded.

To re-read this, please click here. I explained to her that I was the only remaining member of her immediate family and that she would have to move in with me. She's seventeen, I started to say, but he cut me off.

Is she a human being?" he inquired.

After a moment, I nodded.

With an "Alright," he agreed. I think it best if we don't let her near the pack home until she learns more about our kind. We can teach her to behave like a human and help her adjust to the change over time.

After a moment, I nodded.

He turned to me and said, "When is she coming here?"

I said, "In a month.

Alpha Carson inclined his head to one side as he examined me. In other words, "you haven't told me everything."

This caused me to sigh. I said Alpha, "I have to confess to you. My daughter Leah is not thrilled to be here. That much was made obvious by her. To keep her safe, I gave her to her human father while I went in search of a life partner.

Carson, the Alpha, nodded. Do you anticipate that she'll prove to be a source of trouble?" he inquired. He looked at his wolf pack and then back to his eye color. There was a problem.

I said, "I don't know, alpha." "She may be; she tragically lost her dad in a car accident."

I met Alpha Carson's intense gaze. I was taken aback by his unexpected question, "What is that fragrance you're wearing?" My apologies to the leader, I said.

Beta Carson raised his hand. Never mind, he replied. Tell me when you've located her, and I'll post a link to the pack informing the other members of the human's presence on pack territory. You'll have to spread the word about her identity, but I will say that she has to enter school as soon as you learn about our species.

After a moment, I nodded.

Alpha Carson turned to face Julian and greeted him. "You hang back; I want to talk to you about something."

Alpha Carson faced me and flashed a kind grin. Jenny, you may go at any time, he told her.

With a nod, I said farewell and left.

I left the workplace and went back into the world at large.

I set off on foot for the place where I lived.
I wished Leah were here, but my partner was a need.

I headed towards the house my family and I shared and went inside. Walking towards the lounge, I felt the fire's warmth on my face.

Josh, who had been reading quietly on the sofa, glanced up and smiled. He got off the couch and greeted her, "You're home."

I gave him a cheery nod as he walked up to me.

He hugged me tight and drew me to him. His aroma comforts me and puts me at ease.

The wolf within my skull purrs; she's been missing our mate. But, she still pined away for our dog.

Indeed, so did I.

I needed nothing except my loved ones at this time.

Chapter 6

I waited for Jenny to leave the building.

Lynx, my wolf, went crazy at her lovely fragrance. I knew I'd encountered that aroma before, but I couldn't recall where.

I don't know why Lynx wants to take charge, but he won't tell me.

"What's up with you?" I probed him with a query.

Nothing," he snorted, flopping back into my mind. He was becoming even more of a drama princess for me to handle.

When I turned around, I saw that Julian was gazing at me. Jenny's face was awash with honest emotion, and I could read her thoughts and experiences there. The name Julian sprang out of my mouth. If you could tell me the truth, how is Jenny doing right now? And what can you enlighten me about her daughter?

Introducing a person into the group made me nervous. Some of our people are human, yet they're the offspring of wolf pairings.

For me, this was an unusual and peculiar circumstance.

Julian's expression was glum as he looked at me. I'm going to tell you the truth, alpha," he said. She has a very critical daughter. I have firsthand experience with my sister's ordeal since we saw her daily self-destructive behavior right up to the day she confided in us about her hidden family.

It was the worst for me. When Jenny abruptly disappeared without a word, I knew she had met Josh, a human and a close friend of my father's. He lost his mind and began searching the world over for her.

When Julian spoke, I turned to look at him.

'Alpha, Leah didn't want to come here,' he told her. My sister informed me that I had assisted her in getting the judge you described to sign the paperwork we required, and I was astonished to hear that. It was painful to listen to the way her daughter spoke with her.

"What are your expectations?" my Beta, Zain, remarked. Jenny dumped her, so to speak.

Julian hissed, but I revealed my Alpha presence nevertheless, and they immediately bowed to me. I finally said, "Enough."
Inquisitively, I looked at Julian. Zain was correct. There has to be a more effective strategy for Jenny to implement.

I shook my voice clean. Where do your parents stand? Indeed, I did inquire. "Have they come to terms with everything?"

When Jenny had her breakdown and left home, I knew that her parents were furious.

Julian looked at me blankly before he sighed heavily. Julian said, "I spoke to my mom." They'll be back, but it's unclear what they'll do next. My dad, on the other hand, is really angry.

I gave him a blank look.

The parents of both Jenny and Julian are retired old fogies. They were resistant to my leadership since I was so young and didn't have Luna with me when I took over the pack.

She's still evading me, but I have faith that she's alive and well someplace.

I am such an alpha then, but when the time comes, I would want to find my mate.

After glancing at Julian, I sighed. I frowned and replied, "I have a strange feeling this will catch fire in my face." It's hard to fathom why she'd want her kid to visit here. Understanding her feelings for her."

Julian's eyes landed on me.

'I imagine, alpha, she needs a small chance with her,' he moaned. I recall when I first met Larry and how repulsive her feelings for him were. Yet, there was something about him that put my sister & her wolf at rest. I never doubted it for a moment. But I believe Jenny wants to make things up to Leah and herself.

That's a lot more logical. The structure of a generation changes throughout time. My parents are me and our sister, Cassie, when they were the same ages as Jenny because they mated at the same time.

That's OK, I replied. I'll let you go, but tell me when Jenny is coming to get her kid.

I nodded and followed Julian out of the building, leaving Zain and him alone.

Zain sighed as he came over to sit on the chair next to one of my desks. This or that? he mused helplessly. Either human are coming here, or she was told a falsehood about her upbringing. The thought of dealing with werewolves must be overwhelming for her.

True enough.

Because her daughter avoided her, I don't see how she could tell her about us.

I knew I will have to let go, but I couldn't help feeling conflicted.

Honestly, I was at a loss.
When I stared at Zain, I shook my head.

He enquired, "You okay?"

As an answer, I simply laughed. 'I am,' I answered. But I can't say for sure; something seems off. What happened to Jenny's kid is something I just can't seem to get over.

Zaid agreed. 'I get what you're saying,' he replied. Nonetheless, it may be bringing up memories of your father. She indeed went bald around the same time you did.

It could have been because I stared at him. My father was killed by a lone gunman, leaving my mother, sister, and me to fend for ourselves.

I had no problems with Cassie, and I quickly became the pack leader. Josh was instrumental in getting me organized and filing the necessary paperwork. God sent him our way.

My mother, on the other hand, lost her spouse and eventually turned inside. Each night, Cassie and I share a meal with her. She tends to isolate herself from the rest of the pack, seldom leaving her quarters.

The clock told me it was time to depart and meet them for dinner.

I finally responded, "I guess we should get going."

Zaid agreed.

He questioned anxiously, "Is your mom alright today?"

Mom hasn't been out of bed in three days. I told her I'd stay overnight until she found a new place to live. She's eaten, but she hasn't spoken with anybody else. Since it would be unfair to keep constant watch over Cassie, I have just a woman do so.

I sigh.

I reassured her that everything was fine. Cassie seemed to agree that she needs space. The other day was my dad's anniversary.

Zaid agreed.

He raised an eyebrow in my direction and stared at me.

I scowled.
"What?" I got up from my seat and went around the desk to ask. Leave the paperwork where it is; I'll finish up the rest tomorrow.

Zain smiled wryly. He urged me to "get laid" and stated so.

Inaudibly, I groan.

I don't like it when he puts it that way.

Having a good time is the furthest thing from my mind right now. Some girls have come and gone, but they never really did anything for me. This pack's female wolves have tried unsuccessfully to get me to join them, but I haven't. There are a few that I can think of who have tried, but I have avoided them. I frequently only had stands with human beings when I traveled for business or attended Alpha meetings.

Zain got a head shake from me.

As I walked out of my office, I proclaimed, "Not interested." I turned to Zain, who'd been rising from his seat. He glanced at me. Come on, man," he urged. You could lighten up a little. You take everything to heart.

The leader is me, I mumbled. It's a job that never ends, and you know that.

Zain groaned and gave me the eye.

That's exactly what I was thinking," he agreed. But you have to let go every once in a while or you'll go mad stuck within.

When we left the building, I kept my mouth shut. The door was slammed and locked by me.

I directed my amusement squarely at Zain.

What are you doing, exactly? Sometimes though I had a hunch about what he would be up to, I still asked.

Zain snickered.
A little girl wants to share a few real foods with me, he revealed if the truth is known. What happens, happens.

My response was a nod.

The date was headed straight towards someone's bedroom, where we could finally have some of that pleasure he requested me to get.

When I finally spoke out, it was a groan.

Lynx has settled into the minds and is no longer agitated.

As I made my way up the stairs, Zain and I just said our goodbyes.

The sixth floor, where my mother was staying, was the highest point in the building. That was the place she and your father governed the pack from. The studio contained everything you might need.

As I approached the entrance, I took a quick sniff and was pleasantly surprised by the pleasant aroma. I assume the cleaner visited this floor earlier in the day.

As I rang the bell and entered the house, my mom and sister were watching a movie together on the sofa.

The door was locked after I left.

My mom glanced back after me and gave us a teasing grin.

I smiled and replied, "Hello, Mom." The question, "What's on the menu tonight?"

A grin formed on Mun's face.

She proclaimed, "Beef Lasagna." We're talking about "your fave."

When my favorite meal is mentioned, my stomach makes a noise that makes my mom giggle a little.

I have to say that I have missed hearing that laughter during the last several years. We had to take how we can get it, and luckily she was also in a pleasant spirit this evening.

I left the threshold and went to sit in the chair nearby.

My mother and I are both usually required to be with us.

Chapter 7

The two days flew by, and now it's finally here: the day of my father's funeral.

Both the church service and the gathering at Dani's place were intimate.

Everyone came to pay their respects, but I couldn't feel a thing. I gave a slight nod but said nothing else. My thoughts never left my head.

While nobody was looking, I slipped away and sat on Dani's front steps, staring at my own home.

Lucy, who had been following us an around the funeral, sat down next to me after a while, and I knew immediately that she was worried concerning me—but I also knew that her concern was related to my nighttime behavior.

The very first night, I screamed and woke her up, and just last night, I flat-out refused to go to bed. The dream started to affect me. Lucy knew that it stayed in my mind after I told her the first nite, and again the night before.

She asked, "You okay?" as she forced to hand me a drink of wine.

Across the street, I looked at my house.

"I'm okay, I guess," I mumbled, trying to decipher my thoughts.

Without batting an eye, I grabbed the glass from her.

There are many ways to grieve, but for me, I was completely numb and had no idea how to act or feel. Over the past few days, I've spent a lot of time crying, but today I managed to hold it together, with tears coming only during the service.

Lucy was watching me, and I felt her gaze, but I focused on the safety of my home. Did you not sleep again?" she probed.

My head shook.

Lucy reached out and touched my hand. "Leah, I'm worried about you," she expressed concern. Please explain what's bothering you. I will do what I can to assist.

I shut my eyes briefly, then opened them again, knowing I had to share my dream with someone. Things don't make sense, but rather I usually talk to my dad concerning stuff like this, but now I have no one to talk to but myself.

After rubbing my eyes, I looked over at Lucy. She had red, puffy eyes from crying today and clung to my dad. At one point, we even fantasized about becoming sisters if our parents got back together.

I let out a deep sigh. I said, "I keep having such a dream, about the accident," and I turned my eyes away from Lucy, toward the house. I was informed that the incident was an accident and I am aware of its details. My recurring dream, however, is very strange.

I kept talking because I didn't get any responses from Lucy.

As I lay my head on my pillow, I told myself, "The dream begins with us arguing, an argument we had this same night of the crash."

Lucy had been briefed on the dispute and had been asked to keep quiet about it. When I looked at them, a single tear had made its way down my cheek. We were rear-ended, and our car was smashed into from all sides. It was as if I'd been sleeping after getting knocked out, and when I came to, there was someone or something in front of my dad's window. It was human-like in appearance so had yellow eyes but also pointed teeth.

A terrifying mental image appeared, but I quickly dismissed it.

Looking at her, I said, "I awake screaming because every time I can see participants, they have little or no face so I won't recognize them." It felt real, even though I know it can't be real.

Lucy put her head on my shoulder and gave me a tight squeeze.

She said, "Oh, honey." Whatever it means, you should probably talk to someone. Who knows, maybe you're suffering from PTSD.

I remained silent throughout. She wouldn't get it, and I expected that.

A car pulled up and I heard the door open. I backed slowly away and glanced overhead.

My blood began to boil as my attention was drawn to the person before me.

To paraphrase: "Why the hell Why are you on this planet? A shout escaped my lips, and I leaped to my feet. I told you not to come; this is the last place you should be.

When I reached out, Lucy reached out to take my hand.

I can't take my gaze off of my mother.

In front of me, my mother stood.
When someone left the home, she opened her mouth to make a statement though - and quickly closed it again.

Dani, who was standing next to me, yelled, "You heard what Leah replied; you're not welcome here."

My mother looked at both of us, but her attention was clearly on me.

The man on another night broke the silence by warning my mother not to say anything. He'd just gotten out of his car and was approaching my mother.

Another car door opened and closed, drawing my attention to a third man. His gaze followed me, but he never looked away from the car.

Excuse me?

Dani questioned, "Why are you here?" According to the terms of the agreement, "Leah has one month to complete school, or you would collect her."

The man gave Dani a blank look. He turned to Dani and said, "You lied to us." You said Leah still had three weeks of school left, but she appears to have finished all of her coursework and final exams already. A judge friend of mine has ordered that Leah be returned to her mother's custody this evening because her presence here is unnecessary.

Mom just stood there and looked at me.

It's impossible, Dani yelled. To paraphrase: "Not today, at his funeral."

I looked at my mom, but all her attention was on me.

He said, "Leah should pack her things; we'll be leaving soon."

My mother was hugged by the man and they walked away.

I shed a single tear.

"WHY?" I finally broke the impasse by asking.

I shifted my attention from Dani & Lucy to the stranger and my mother. Without actually looking at us, I could tell the man was watching. 'Why now?' I questioned. After all those years, you still didn't want to find out. You abandoned me.
I could no longer take it. I said, my rage filling every pore of my body, "I'm not a thing you're able to pick up any time you feel like it."

I confronted them directly and glared.

My mother was being comforted when a man out of the car came over.

Something about the way he held her caught my attention, and I stared at them.

The realization then hit me like a ton of bricks: his tender grip on her was reminiscent of the way my father would hold her. My dad gave her that look of endearment all the time.

The words came out of my mouth and I looked at her.

Both my mother and the other man tensed up.

My thoughts were racing through my head like a time machine.

Though the realization initially slowed me down, I was aware.

The words "it was him" from my lips in a hushed whisper. You dumped my dad on him, she said.

My mother suddenly said, "You don't understand," and made a move toward me, which caused me to retreat.

It bothered me to have her close by.

My mother gave me a teary-eyed look. She was about to burst into tears, so she can't be serious now.
I scowled.

You abandoned my Dad for that, I said. And why is it that you couldn't bring me along or even visit me? Is it that he just didn't want you?

I tried to tough it out, but the pain was too much. My head felt heavier and heavier. My eyes had to close because of the pain in my head.

I sensed the approach of arms.

She called me "Leah," but I avoided her.

Leave me alone! I yelled.

As the pain increased, I instinctively reached for my head. I just had to let out a yell.

I didn't know what the hell must have been going on.

I felt my legs go weak and clutched my head. I felt like my body was on fire and I had no command over it.

I just keeled over and gave up.

I thought I heard a yell of "LEAH," but it was difficult to determine who it came from.

I hit the ground hard, and as my eyes began to close in shock, I saw my mother and or the two men peering at me in disbelief.

Within seconds, all light had vanished from my world.

Chapter 8

Astounded, I just stared.

Leah fell to the ground, clutching her throbbing head.

Everyone in the house rushed outside to surround her, but again the woman still glared at me.

"Look at what you've done!" she said.

A call for an ambulance was audible in the background.

Josh reassured me by keeping his arm over my shoulders. To soothe my wolf, he would have to come to me. She didn't agree about what Leah said and decided to take charge.

I don't understand how she made the connection between Josh and me. She was never around when I was seeing him, I realized. She probably wouldn't remember that far back, but there was that one time he showed up.

The woman yelled at me again, ripping me out of my thoughts, "You need to leave now."

As the sirens approached, I turned and stood still.

As I watched the ambulance rush to my daughter, I couldn't muster any emotion. Whoa, what the heck was going on with her?

I was curious, but she disliked me so much that no one would tell me the truth. In their eyes, I was the villain.

There was a bridging of minds.

We're going to bring her back to the pack, Julian said. There, the medic in charge of the pack can examine her.

Initially, I was nervous.

It piqued my interest to learn if we should.

Behind me stood the house where I had raised my children before meeting my current partner.

The only people who overheard me say, "I need to go there," were Julian and Josh.

Julian followed my gaze and nodded.

He made a U-turn and finally followed his calling as a lawyer.

He asked Dani to "pack all of Leah's belongings," but was met with a smack from Leah's roommate. An angry "I won't do anything for you" came back at him from her mouth.

Julian gave her a curious look.

Through the mental link, he said, "This human does indeed have balls; I give wife that."

I sensed Josh's sense of humor through our mate connection, and he agreed.

When I turned around, I saw Leah being carried off on a stretcher. The ambulance was approaching and she was being brought in.

When reminded, Julian said, "Oh, I forgot," and moved closer to Dani. They'll be taking Leah by ambulance to the local hospital, he said.

The woman returned his glare. I will report the smack you gave me as assault if you don't pack some stuff for her.

Julian gave her the ruling paper we had drafted for her.

Julian discovered the lady and my daughter had fabricated an excuse for missing school. Julian informed me about it yesterday. That didn't shock me at all. Before relocating, I had assumed that Leah would like to see her pals one last time. She was brilliant and doing well in all of her studies, Julian claimed, so her father did not doubt that she had passed. She may finish school this year.

And I was so pleased with myself.

To clarify, Julian made some phone calls, and we visited Alpha Carson. We'd been having difficulties with another pack and some rogues, and he insisted that Leah stay on pack territory.

I then snapped out of it and looked at the woman.

The lady stood still and just nodded her head.

A lady who seemed to be around the same age as Leah hurried up and embraced her. It was a pleading, "Mother, please," but she was having none of it. She doesn't want to go, and neither does Leah.

The woman's eyes met mine, and while her glare was present, her expression was one of defeat.

The lady sighed as she studied the paper. She said softly, "There's nothing I can do." It was obvious that she adored my kid.

We're coming over to your house," Julian said.
The lady seemed startled and shot me a glare.

Her gaze never left mine as she said, "You honestly believe she wants to cross that bridge." It's the way you parted ways many years ago. Larry remained unchanged because he was too busy caring for Leah.

As she spoke, I felt a tightening in my chest.

Even while standing on all fours, my wolf let out a whimper.

The lady looked at me curiously before reaching into her pocket. She produced an item and lobbed it in my direction. Here's the answer," she said.

I was allowed to leave, and Josh came back to get it.

Let's go, he said, his voice low and close to mine.

My response was a nod.

I turned away from the gathering and walked back home.

As soon as I stepped outdoors, I had to stop and look at it. Is everything well, Josh questioned.

I remained silent throughout.

From the street, the home seemed unchanged.

As I approached the house, Josh inserted the key into the ignition and unlocked the door.

I can smell them now.

We're talking about Larry and Leah here.

When I shut my eyes, all of the times we had together came rushing back to me.

Tears streaming down my cheeks, I opened them.

Josh's arm was on the small of my tail as he ushered me inside.

That lady wasn't lying; the interior of the house did appear to be unchanged as well. This is how it looked when we first moved in and decorated.

I stopped where I was and stared at myself, trying to take it all in.

The home had been meticulously cleaned, but some items were still misplaced.

The picture frames on the mantel caught my eye.

I came forward and took a position in front.

None of the pictures included me; they all happened after I left.

It broke my heart, and yet I knew I must have hurt them by doing that.

I kept still while Josh and Julian went on a search.

And then I heard Julian say, "The house documents must be here," and turned to look at him over my shoulder. No, I responded.

Both Julian and Josh were staring at me.

It's time for her to go, Jen. Julian replied, but I gave him a grunt in response. "Don't. Just get out of here!

Julian gave me a look, but Josh came on first. He called me "sweetheart" as I gazed at him. I gave a little shake of the head, and he shut his mouth. The only thing sally has left of him is that ring, and I didn't want to take that from her. Saying, "I just can't,"

I separated myself from them and glanced between them. "It pained her that I abandoned her," I sobbed. She's in pain because I chose you.

When I looked at Josh, his expression relaxed. I looked around the home and said, "I can't." I opened them and did look at Josh, who was staring intently at me, and warned him, "This might hurt you." If I knew Larry, he'd put all of his debts in her name even before I moved out of this place that used to be my home. If she doesn't want to do it, I won't force her to. We're moving out, so the house is available for rent. With a tear in my eye, I said, "But this house is Leah's," and I moved closer to Josh and put my hand in his. After a year, she'll be old and capable of living on her own, and I sighed, "We only have a wife for a year." She can't live with the pack anymore, therefore she needs a new home.
When he nodded, Josh clasped my hand.

He turned to Julian and remarked, "That sounds like a simpler plan." You need to make sure that everything is legal and that the rental is available for a full year so that Leah may return if she so chooses.

As the truth dawned on him, Julian nodded.

To which I said, "I never thought of it that way," and he glanced at me. "Jen, that's a smart plan. The judge and every other person will be getting support from me.

A moment later, Josh noticed somebody knocking at the line and started to let whoever was there in.

It was the same young lady as before.

I looked at her blankly for a moment.

"Here," she responded, producing a tote. My mom gathered them for Leah's stay with us the other night.

When Josh accepted the bag, I gave him the okay.

While she studied me, the little girl chewed her lower lip. I recognized that expression; she wanted to say something. I got in closer and studied her carefully. She sighed and continued to stare at me. "You should know, Leah hasn't been sleeping particularly well since the disaster; Elizabeth has been screaming and has even had insomnia," she said. "I have higher hopes for you now."

I gave her a slight nod and a grin. "Thank you for informing me," I said.

The girl returned my gaze and flashed me a shy grin. However, she did sneak a peek indoors. She said with a tear rolling down her cheek, "We used a lot of fun." It was great having Leah here.

Her gaze returned to mine. She said, "I realize you have your reasons for leaving." "At first, Leah was always raving about you, but as time went on, she stopped bringing you up altogether. You were dead, and she let everyone know it.

I felt bad for Leah, but I understood her perspective.

The young lady sighed.

She responded, "I know she needs to leave." But, will she be able to stay in touch? I loved her like a sister.

I gave a slight nod and a friendly smile.

I told her that I would make sure she got in touch with you.

She gave a curt nod and walked away.

Once she had left, Josh locked the door.

As Julian leaned against the kitchen counter, he complimented the girl. It's too bad her mother is such a nut.

Having completed my circle, I scowled at him. Then I responded, "Really."

Julian smiled as he started to speak but was interrupted by his phone. When Julian's phone rang, he reached into his pocket and responded to it.
He waits a few seconds, then shuts it. I catch his eye. A medical transport vehicle had already arrived, he informed them. "At this point, Leah is being returned to the pack. That we may finally return to our homes."

My response was a nod.

I seemed to be searching for something when something caught my peripheral vision. I made my way over and saw a picture of Leah along with another girl with their hands on a trophy. I took it and gave Josh another glance. I'd like to amass more presents for her. When will it be acceptable to leave? Indeed, I did inquire.

Josh confirmed with a nod.

"I'll go get the car," he promised. Just throw everything in a bag and hand it to us; we'll load the car.

I gave a brief nod and headed upward.

I went to her room because I thought maybe she never left.

Leah's room has not changed since she was a newborn.

As soon as I walked in, I could smell her. As my inner wolf surveys the scene, she emits a soothing purr of approval.

"Pup was good," she said, taking in the various awards and songbirds.

I had to concede that she had probably competed in and won every imaginable topic and athletic competition there was.

I went over to her room and accessed her wardrobe. I grabbed a bag from my closet and began stuffing it with clothes.

After she had finished packing, I found a picture that showed her and her dad when she was 9.

When I saw how joyful she seemed, I couldn't help but grin. I put it in the suitcase.
There was one stuffed animal on her freshly made bed.

I took it and grinned at it.

She still had the teddy bear I gave her before she was born.

I stacked it atop the other items I'd snatched.

Josh's familiar aroma wafted in through the open door, and I recognized him immediately.

With a question, "Is this all?" he listened intently.

I peered over her shoulder at him, as his gaze searched the room in enjoyment. Wow, he exclaimed. "She can enjoy games, and it appears she was nice as well, so the boys will romance her."

I smiled.

"I know," I say: ". We're bringing the bag and all the extras on top. Please have someone bring sheets to cover the furnishings.

Josh confirmed with a nod.

"Julian is staying over for a few nights; he wants to tidy up the house," he remarked as a gradual smile itched his face. "But I believe he loves getting under another woman's skin more."

"I sighed.

Even though he was single, my brother would play a field with everyone who moved.

I hope he is doing this correctly.

Josh and I traveled out of Leah's hallway, however as I closed the entrance, I can indeed resist checking in one last glimpse.

We went downstairs after I locked the door behind us.

Julian offered to remain behind to make sure the home was in order. He planned to return after a short time to wrap up his business.

I gave him a hug and a nod.

Josh and I headed to the vehicle and hopped in. Everyone here was evaluating me, and I could feel their gaze, so I lowered my head. I didn't want my wolf to have to deal with any more stress, so I avoided it.

My werewolf huffed in approval.

I leaned back against the seat.

The truth dawned on me: I was taking Leah back to my place.

I was necessary to be her mom now.

With a sigh, I watched Josh pull away.

We left the lane and were supposed to head toward where the emergency room was waiting.

I leaned back on my bar stool, knowing I would have my family back.

I hope Leah can excuse me for what I did, so that we may slowly move forward and with restoring what we can.

Chapter 9

While I listen to Julian mostly on the phone, I glanced forward and fixed my eyes on Zain. I mumbled an "okay" in response. Be sure to get back to us by Saturday.

I finished my call and checked my Beta.

We're almost there," I told her, referring to Jenny and Josh's return. The human had an emotional breakdown, and an ambulance is taking her to the packing hospital.

Zain agreed with a grimace on his face. He enquired, "What occurred?"

Defeated, I let out a sigh.

They must have walked in on the burial, and Julian, being Julian, probably made a huge speech, I said. "She was anxious and probably right that Mommy left Dad for Josh," the author writes.

Zain looked at me with disbelief.

He questioned, "How the heck did she figure it out?"

I said, "I have no idea; neither would Jenny and Julian."

A sigh escaped Zain's lips.

Awful creature, he sighed. The previous several days have been particularly trying for her.

That got a yes from me.

I had to concede that he was right.

I sighed as I glanced at the clock.

I said, "We received training."

To which Zain gave a resounding yes.

We got up from our seats and Zain and I exited the office.

Every day, we have training.
The following day, when Jenny or Julian returned from human settlement, the pack grounds were assaulted by rogues.

The bad guys were eliminated, leaving just 10 survivors. It's a relief that nobody was hurt. I was on edge since the assault seemed to come out of nowhere. The criminals seemed to be on the prowl for anything or someone.

I instituted a stringent lockdown procedure for the pack.

I recall Julian bursting in and pleading for permission to go retrieve Leah with Jenny and Josh. I was skeptical at first, but he assured me that the girl or a lady had lied to them about her not being able to finish school when in fact she had. In the end, I decided to agree with you. My confidence in a lockdown's ability to protect my pack let Lynx and me relax.

I didn't get my footing until Julian explained the strategy to me. The pack includes Julian, who is also a lawyer. A witch friend of ours helped him out by concocting a potion to mask his aroma. Just in case, he brought some along for the rest of them. Unfortunately, I didn't know it was the father's funeral when I had them depart yesterday night.

When Zain and I approached the pack training area, we saw that everyone had already been there.

I knew everyone was but anyway Josh and Jenny since I had forbidden them to leave the group.

When Zain and I observed, I signaled the trainer to begin.

While I generally exercise with everyone else, I wanted to make sure everyone was obeying the rules this time.

A she-wolf with a sneer on her face was watching me, and I could feel her eyes on me.

I scowled.

I turned to see Zain chuckling to himself. 'Man,' I said. "She needs to be in training. Get your sex life in order thereafter.

A sigh escaped Zain's lips. He insisted that "you certainly need some." For her and their friend Rachel, I was planning a little party.

In a low voice, I snarled.

What the f*ck, I yelled. No she-wolves will catch me banging them.

Zain made a surrender sign with his hands. A muffled "I'm sorry" came out of his mouth. He started to say, "I didn't intend to...," but the sound of approaching sirens stopped him short.

I happened to glance across and saw an ambulance arrive at the animal hospital.
There was a complete halt in activity as everyone gazed.

In a low voice, I snarled.

I ordered them to "go back to training." "You won't find anything interesting here."

Everyone resumed their training sessions.

When I glanced at Zain, Come on, I urged them. Jenny and Josh have also just arrived. Check on everyone and make sure they're all OK.

With a nod, Zain and I left.

Lynx was already on red alert & pacing as we got closer to the ambulance.

What's the matter? I inquired of him, but he paid me no mind.

Oh no, he's back to his odd behavior.

As I entered the hospital, Jenny was standing there with a doctor, both of them visibly shaken. She implored, "Please let me see her.

I approached them on foot. How are things?" I inquired.

As the door toward the room opened, the overwhelming aroma that flooded out struck me like a tonne of bricks. Lavender was there in the air.

The doctor was speaking, but I couldn't understand a word. I focused intently on the entrance.

I shook my head in response to Lynx's roar.

Just what did you say? I consulted the physician.

The doctor gave me a wry smile before sighing.

She had a brain injury in the crash, he added. She was in such much discomfort that I decided to put her in an unconscious state for the time being.
That got a yes from me.

"What's going to happen?" As I made my way toward the exit, I inquired.

We're going to scan her, and then we'll know what to do," he said.

Jenny mumbled, "Alright.

I turned to look at her, but she had already turned her attention back to the door I had been gazing at.

She whimpered, "They won't let me see her," and avoided my gaze as she said it.

Josh yelled, "Sweetheart!" Mommy, the boys yelled to Alec and Ethan.

Jenny gave a shake of her head and began to cry.

As I was attempting to piece together what the heck had just happened to me, Josh walked over to his girlfriend and consoled her.

I turned my attention back to Lynx, who was looking concerned. What's the matter? Indeed, I did enquire. He started to speak, but the aroma interrupted him.

Two nurses were shoving a bed out of the way as I turned around to watch. Seeing her lying there on the bed like that reminded me of an angel.

Lynx yelled, "Mate."

Incredulous, I stared back at him.

"Mate," he shouted.

When the nurses carted her away, I cast my gaze toward the bed.

Her skin was ghostly white, but I recognized her instantly.

When they rounded the bend, I kept an eye on them.

My murmured "mate" was heard by him.

A gasp erupted, but I continued staring at the bed.

Inquiring, "What did you say?" Jenny pressed on.
I blew her off while licking my lips. When I turned around, I saw them wheeling her away.

I shook my voice clean. "Cheapskate," I referred to myself as.

As I turned around, Jenny was approaching me and examined my face. She looked at my face and said, "You sure?"

I frowned and nodded my head.

I answered "yes." While she was being brought out, Lynx "called mate."

Jenny looked downcast as I fixed my gaze on her.

She took a few steps back and shook her head at me while saying, "NO, NO, NO." "I just got her back, and she's my daughter."

My eyes landed on her. Their offspring?

Suddenly I realized that the ambulance probably included her daughter. Jenny came back to the house the other day and must have picked up some of her perfume since it was in there.

It explains Lynx's peculiar behavior.

Josh murmured, "Alpha Carson," and I snapped out of my reverie.

When I looked at him, he looked at me.

A single word: "Alpha," he said. She doesn't realize she's here, so she's angry when she wakes up, and she and Jenny need some time to get back on track, so you might be forced to wait.

I scowled.

Josh touched my shoulder and looked at me intently. I know she's your soul match, he added. Yet she doesn't know who we are, and she just recently lost her dad. She'll be a hot mess. You have to be patient with her and try to act humanely at first.

Lynx moaned and stood still. I could see he was eager to meet her, but there was a delay.

Jenny was scated in a chair, crying onto a nurse's shoulder as they tried to console her.

Defeated, I let out a sigh.

"I know," I affirmed. I like to observe from a safe distance till the dust settles.

Jenny raised an eyebrow and smiled knowingly at me.

I was sorry for her, but I could see this would be difficult with Lynx present.

Jenny and I sat down close to one other.
Everyone scattered to various chairs around the lobby.

I stretched out my neck and leaned against the wall.

Jenny reassured herself, "She'll be alright," and she muttered it. I swiveled around to face her. We made eye contact. "She was upset that I wasn't giving her a whole month with your buddy," she said, her eyes dropping. Because she was already upset with me, she may still not want to have any contact with me.

I reached out and touched hers, beaming at her.

I assured her that she would be OK. Didn't you tell them once that it takes time for everything to mend, even the other stuff?

Jenny looked at me intently and nodded. Her lips curved into a tinier grin. She said, "You recalled."

That got a yes from me.

I was a wreck when my dad died, so I took out into the woods. Jenny found me by the lake after everyone had looked for me, and we sat there together. She never once tried to contact anybody to let them know I was okay. Jenny heard me bawl and go on about how much I missed my dad. But then it struck me: Jenny looked like she'd lost a loved one, and now that I think about it, she had lost a daughter.

I was returned to me by Jenny, and Josh aided me in carrying my baggage. Yet, Jenny returned home after that night and never looked back. No one knew why she did it, but everything made sense now that she had.

Jenny brushed her tears away and stared wide-eyed at the hospital door. Her parents were standing in the direction she was staring.

Mother, she said softly. "Dad."

They took a glance around and then focused on me. Both of them bowed respectfully. It was a collective "Alpha" that they said.

I gave a little nod but remained silent.

Jenny's mom came up and put her hand in Jenny's. A hushed "I'm sorry, Jen" escaped her lips. How is she feeling?

Jenny just shrugged and didn't respond.

Josh filled them in on the details. Jenny's mother sat across from her, while her father leaned against the wall, his expression bland but indicating something. He seemed worried, but there was more going on. Lynx himself was at a loss to explain.

Zain stared at me specifically as we sat around chatting. He turned to the side, then returned to me, and added, "I instructed everyone that training would resume at that exact time day after day henceforth."

After hearing what he did, I knew he would want to talk about it. I connected with him mentally.

I informed him, "She's my mate." He made no expression at all. I need your assistance with her. I have no notion what I should be doing.

He vowed, "I will." I need to get some paperwork done, so off to the office, I go. Maybe I can learn more about her by poking around through the materials that Julian has provided us.

I looked right at him and he grimaced. He intended to learn about her interests and hobbies.

I mumbled an "okay" in response. Don't tell anybody; I'm having trouble claiming them as it is.

Zain agreed and disconnected.

The stillness had returned.

Everyone was concerned about her, but no one could pinpoint the source of their worries.

Chapter 10

After an hour, I have yet to meet the doctor or our companion.

I had become careless.

Lynx was nervously pacing.

While I watched the hall, I became aware of some activities. Our previous doctor appeared and made his way over to us.

I sat up upright.

The doctor halted in front of her and looked directly at Jenny.

"Leah is fine," he reassured her. She's doing OK now."

What did your scan reveal? Jenny stood forward and questioned.

The doctor gave Jenny his whole focus after giving her his partial attention for a few seconds. The scan revealed no abnormalities. Neither the collapse nor the events you described are within our ken.

Jenny sobbed softly and returned to her seat.

I glanced at the doctor.

"Have you thought about how this may have occurred?"

I was the focus of his "I don't know" as he looked at me. I would have thought a brain hemorrhage, although there was no indication of it. On the scan, there was no evidence.

He caught my gaze but then turned to Jenny. How much rest has Leah been getting lately?

Jenny's eyes widened as I looked at her, and she nodded reassuringly.

'I forced her to consider moving with me,' she whimpered. Before we departed, her companion said that she, too, had been having trouble sleeping. Was that me?

As I turned my head again, the doctor was shaking his.

The doctor said, "No, I do not think so; I just will need to find out why or if anything had changed in her life, but I consider the sleep deprivation can't improve; it'll all rely heavily on how little sleep Helen has been knowing, and put a lot of pressure on the highest part of it all, just not rolling to this location but the failure of her father, which could have helped cause this, and though we don't know how this happened, we ought to keep her there for a few days."

I gave him a startled look.

There were things I suspected, but I wasn't going to tell them. Lynx groaned, but he also seemed to agree with my thoughts.

Jenny was dead set on seeing her, thus it's possible that her actions contributed to the overall reason. Because she had already made plans to see the father, I knew she was planning on returning her first. They got together, and he said he'd speak to Leah if she wanted to, but he left the decision up to her. Jenny consented, but things changed when she got a call first from the hospital informing her of the incident and the deaths of her old girlfriend. Both scared and curious, she wants to visit.

A social worker came waiting for her, and she was told that Leah, being just seventeen, had to move into an older relative, even though a friend was willing to do so. Jenny was at her wit's end and needed some guidance, so she reached out to Julian and me for support.

I thought it was best for Leah to stick with familiar faces, but Jenny was curious about whether or not she would fit in with the pack. Although her kid was a human who was unaware of us, I was hesitant to ask. I was astonished when Julian said an old packmate resided near the human village, but he did remark there had been a lot of twisting and tossing.

The older member of the pack explained to me that she may join the pack, but she would have to make a loyalty oath to us and promise never to speak about our species to other humans. He also said that Jenny could file out paperwork to reclaim her kid and that we could keep track of human occupancy to adhere to regulations.

Julian accomplished everything and even created the paperwork to show it was legal.

I gave the doctor a puzzled look and shook my head.

Asking, "What do we do now?" Indeed, I did enquire.

The physician heaved a sigh. He reassured her that all she needed to do was get some sleep and that she'd be back to normal in no time.
Once he got my sign of OK, the doctor headed back down the hall.

I cast my eyes across the assembled waiters. I finally spoke out and suggested we all go home and get some shut-eye.

Jenny mumbled, "I want to remain."

That's why I thought about it.

I said, "No." With all that's occurred, Jen needs to take it easy and get some rest, so please tell her to do that, Jen.

Jenny turned to me but said nothing.

Josh approached her and put a comforting hand on her back. Jenny turned to gaze at him when he stated, "Alpha Carson is correct." Leah must get some sleep. She needs to relax after what has transpired; the doctor is on his way over.

Jenny frowned, "She is going to be on her own," as she surveyed the group.

It's not going to happen, I told her. She has to be able to trust someone, so I'll remain for a bit, but I believe it's better if the doctor speaks to her first.

I heard a voice ask, "What about me?" and turned to find my sister, Cassie, standing there.

I scowled.

"What?" Indeed, I did enquire. What were you thinking?

Cassie shrugged.
She looked at everyone and remarked, "I believe she may feel secure with somebody of her age." If she wakes, I can chat with her or possibly be her buddy, so I can remain here while visitors all sleep.

I looked at her and moaned in frustration.

Once the doctor came back into the room, I responded, "Fine."

I finally got his attention by calling him "Dr."
"Alpha."

We're going to go ahead and go ahead and get some sleep, but I need you to let Jenny and me know as soon as she wakes up. "Cassie will join you here."

The doctor confirmed this by nodding.

The group lingered for a few minutes before dispersing one by one, leaving me alone with Cassie & Jenny. Once the lads departed, Josh walked out again to wait on Jenny alone until the doctor and her parents arrived.

We were just about to leave when we heard a bed being pushed, so I turned around to see the nurses wheeling Leah's bed back into the room.

My stomach did a little flip as I got sight of her.

Lynx was nearby but remained unseen at all times.

When they were putting her in place, Jenny and I headed towards the entrance, and then we went inside to have a look. Leah looked like a little doll lying on the bed.

The bandage on her head prevented me from getting a good look at her face.

The doctor entered and immediately began taking her vitals. When he was finished, he turned to us and flashed a kind grin. He recommended that the two of them go. A nurse will be checking her at a regular hour.

That got a yes from me.

The door closed once the doctor left.
Jenny circled the bed and stopped at the foot, where she regarded her from below. Her feelings permeated the room and I could sense them. When she was 3, I started singing to her," she said softly.

I briefly met her gaze before returning them to my partner.

Sniff, Jenny.

As she continued, "You have to win the girl over like a person," I turned to look at her.

Jenny persisted as I stiffened. She insisted that I take her out on dates to know her. "The conventional approach."

I kept my mouth shut.

Jenny moaned as she turned back to me and then to Leah. I became acquainted with her father, and my wolf had nothing but good things to say about him, she added. Two months before giving birth, I found out I was pregnant.

Jenny glanced at me, but there was more going on.

Her head trembled, but she quickly shifted the topic.

She turned and left, saying, "I will allow you to enjoy a few minutes alone with her; I believe we each require a bit of sleep."

She started towards the exit, but all I could do was gaze at my partner.

After Jenny left, I went over to stand in her place.

As I placed my palm in hers, electricity began to course through my body.

It was obvious that she was the one for me.

My mum gave me a checklist of things to consider while looking for a life partner. The wolf's strange behavior, the tingles I felt, and even the smell she left behind were all the results of my mate.

Lynx inched closer and fixed his gaze on our partner. He let himself a little whimper. His sadness is washing over me.

That was a whiny "Mate" from him.
It hurt me to see him suffer.

I needed her to wake up, but I also had to play my cards well.

I whispered, "Lynx," and he turned to look at me. We must take care of our partners properly. We need to go on dates with her or get to know her better. But we will be there, even if it means spending every night in a tent outside her door. I believe in us.

I can't remember whether I was attempting to persuade him or myself.

Lynx met my gaze directly.

With a sigh of exasperation, he takes a few steps back. He has settled inside my brain and is staring at me. He finally conceded, "Fine, we do that method."

That got a yes from me.

I cocked my head to the side and leaned toward my partner. I kissed her cheek and felt a flutter of excitement.

When I came closer, I could smell her all over me. The aroma caused my mouth to start watering.

I withdrew a step and released her hand.

Slowly, I turned my gaze away from her.

I headed in that direction and unlocked the door. When I passed through it, it shut securely behind me. I turned to see the nurse staring at me from her position beside the entrance.

"Alpha," she murmured.

After giving a brief nod, I started to go.

Till I heard her awake, I knew I couldn't go to sleep. But after that... I had the notion, "She has no idea who I am."

I left the clinic and made my way to the storage facility.

I wanted to sit down, have a drink, and plan my next move.

Chapter 11

Even as the night engulfed me, I had a sense that I was secure.

My back felt comfortable on whatever I was sitting on.

Not being with Dani and Lucy was obvious, but there were still some mysteries.

Someone leaned in and kissed me on the cheek, but who could it have been? I felt tingles go through my body like an electric current. I was aware of a musky, though unidentifiable aroma.

I froze; I couldn't even bring myself to gaze at the sky.

After what seemed like hours, I made a little movement and opened my eyes. The blurriness cleared up after I blinked just a few times. After regaining my equilibrium, I cast my gaze outside.

I wasn't with Dani and Lucy, but I was somewhere.

There were tubes coming out of me and equipment on each side of me when I glanced around and at my hands.

I'm at a medical facility, but where is everyone?

There was some motion outside, and I could feel the door crack open. A lady carrying a tray entered, but she paused when she saw that I was awake. "You're awake?" she said in apparent amazement.

I shook my voice clean. "I must be lost." Sleepily, I inquired.

The lady gave me a little grin as she gazed at me. At the hospital, she informed him. I'll have the doctor call you right immediately.

I looked at her intently, but she abruptly turned and walked away.

I figured she must have been the nurse.

My head felt heavy, so I leaned back against the cushion. As I put my hand over my head, I felt bandages. What the heck went wrong here?

I felt the terror rising inside of me.

Someone opened the door and a male and a younger girl around my age came in.

"I'm Doctor Reed," the medical professional introduced himself. They were scared of you.

What occurred? While I wanted to inquire, my question came out all sandpapery. I was parched. It was then that I licked his lips.
After staring at me for just a few seconds, Doctor Reed's companion moves past him to the table's other side. On the table was a glass of water along with a small cup.

I kept a tight eye as she filled the little cup with water and set the jug back down. She circled back around, stepped up to where I was lying, and brought the cup up to my mouth. To this, he said, "Have a taste," smiling slightly.

I followed her instructions and took a drink, but once the water went into my throat, I shut my eyes and braced myself for the shock of cold.

After what seemed like an eternity, I finally opened my eyes & glanced there at the girl, but before that glanced at the doctor, who was smiling. "Are you doing better?" he queried.

I nodded my head weakly, which just made things worse; the small pain in my head caused me to shut my eyes once more.

"Oh," he mumbled. Certainly not me!

As the sharp agony had gone, I cautiously opened my eyes and gazed back at them, but he persisted. Maybe you had a concussion. We ran scans to check for brain abnormalities but found none. He assured me, "All you need is some rest, and you'll be fine."

I just looked, both bewildered and alarmed.

"I must be lost." I finally found my voice and asked.

After staring at mine for a while, the doctor finally said. The young lady informed me, "You're in the hospital." You passed out in the car as your mother drove you to this from your hometown.

I turned to peer at the young lady who had spoken.

As my mom was brought up, I felt a wave of rage wash over me, but I held it back. I was feel a little weak and my head ached.

Can you tell me where she is? As coolly as I could, I inquired.

The girl gave me a grin as she gazed at me. She added, "She's sleeping but she'll be here shortly."

I looked at her incomprehensively before shifting my focus to the doctor. "I don't want to see her," I finally said.

I observed the doctor's frown form as he continued to gaze. I can't prevent your mom from visiting, he added. So get some sleep; you may see her once you feel better.

I scowled.

From what you've stated, I gathered that she abducted me against my will. "I have no interest in meeting her."

The physician seemed perplexed but made no expression.

A few moments later, he turned around and nodded. "I will tell her nurse to keep her out," he promised. He glanced at me. She was a hot mess after you were hauled in, however, she never left the side until we forced you to go so we could check your vitals, so I believe you should connect with her.

When I looked at him, he looked at me. I can't decide whether I should trust him or slap him. If she did, it didn't matter to me; I didn't want to be in it.

There was a noticeable void of conversation in the room.

The physician swallows hard. He turned on his heel and walked out of the room, saying, "Well, I have other customers to visit."

As soon as the door had closed behind him, my focus shifted to the girl.

During my conversation with the doctor, she kept staring at me. I scowled.

What's your name? Indeed, I did enquire. No, I don't recognize you.

When she said, the girl cracked a grin. That's an "I know that, foolish" she said. "Hi, I'm Cassie, and I'm a local girl. Your mom is a close friend of mine, so I'm familiar with her.

I could not take my eyes off her.

I couldn't make sense of it.

"What are you doing here?" Indeed, I did enquire. For an instant, Cassie cocked her head downward and studied me. You remind me of your mother. And her eyes are just like his," he remarked.

I kept my mouth shut.

My whole appearance, save for my eyes, was inherited from my dad. They resembled my mothers in every way.

Cassie heaved a sigh and scooted closer to the chair. She sat down, and I stared at her in disbelief.

She sat back in her chair and remarked, "I thought you might use a buddy." I was expecting you to say something like, "I'd rather be at home."

The devil knows how she could have known that. Do people in this little town just love to spread rumors, or did my mum just prefer to speak about her private life?

She suddenly says, "I believe you should give your mom a chance," and I snap out of my reverie.

I just stared at her in disbelief.

The young lady shook her head. When she said, "I don't mean you can forgive her," she wasn't implying that. Let her explain herself, please. You have no idea why she went; you were never close to her.

Is that so? Inquired I of her directly.

Cassie looked at me thoughtfully for a while before shrugging. She said, "I don't know." It's not my narrative to share even if I did know what happened.

She had figured out why.

I averted my gaze and focused on the wall in front of me.

I'm in an unfamiliar area with a lady I haven't spoken to in eight years and don't want to see again.

I had no idea how I could want out of this jam.
I overheard Cassie say in a whisper, "You know she seems to have a family."

My eyes landed on her.

My mom was part of a nuclear family.

When the details of my father's burial came flooding back to me, I closed my eyes.

There was the guy from the previous night, as well as another male. He loved my mum and looked at her with such warmth.

Surely it was her significant other.

I had a hunch he was, but I couldn't shake the feeling that I'd seen him somewhere before. But I can't say for sure where.

Leah!, yelled Cassie. A tear escaped and I blinked them open. My eyes shifted to hers. Her eyes held a multitude of feelings, but in recent days, the one I recognized best was pity.

I shook my voice clean. I rolled over away from her and said, "I guess I need to sleep."

There were tears in my eyes, but I never showed them.

When he wasn't around, I felt empty.

I needed him to come back into my life.

She decided to remain in the area, as she said. I hope everything is ok with you.

I kept my mouth shut.

I focused on the wall in front of me and let the tears fall softly.

The pain in my head had subsided, but a haze had obscured my vision.

I tried to enter a trance by shutting my eyes and letting my body fall into darkness, but the yellow eyes were waiting for me once again.

When will this recurring dream end?

Chapter 12

When exactly I dozed off is beyond me, but I awakened with a start.

The walls in front of mine caught my attention. I had to blink many times. In a leisurely motion, I rolled onto my back. As I was falling onto my back, I caught sight of something out of the window of my vision.

As I turned around, my mother was there, but Cassie was nowhere to be seen.

My mother was gazing at me, but when I met her gaze, her eyes widened and she stepped closer, prompting me to take a few steps back. My mother pauses a wave of pain sweeping over her.

Her hushed "Sorry" caught my attention and I turned to look at her. When I looked her over, I saw that her eyes seemed bloodshot despite her pale complexion.

My mother looked at me quizzically for a while before clearing her throat. It's all quite fresh to you, she acknowledged. I didn't feel like doing any of this.

I looked at her in disbelief.

When she was talking to me, Mom never took her gaze off of me. I'm sorry I abandoned you was the last thing she said. Something occurred, and I became someone I never imagined myself to be in the past.

I scowled.

My wrath caused me to say, "So that meant leaving your kid alone without knowing wherever you went."

As a youngster, I didn't give a damn about her since she abandoned me. That's something no mother would ever do to her kid.

I sat up in bed, but I kept staring at my mom's face the whole time. Her face contorted in apparent perplexity. She starts to say, "I instructed your father to warn you..." but I interrupt her. I said, "No." He said you had called and wanted to meet me, but I declined to be informed. I didn't want to run into you.

My mom stiffened, shifted in her seat, and gave me the cold shoulder. She said that her new perspective was the result of being apart for so long. Things were more difficult than they are now, yet I could have done more. I was hoping your dad would fill you in on certain details.

I just stood there and gaped at her. That's how ignorant she was; when she dumped me, I didn't hear from her for 9 years and never found out why.

She finally opened up to her friend, saying, "Leah, I wanted to speak to you; I was curious about everything there is about my life." Never did I want to be apart from you. I never expected to be in this position. I always imagined I'd end up with your dad, but then fate pushed me into the middle of something that completely altered my course.

The words "your lover" sprang out of my mouth.

Mom was staring at me.

To which he said, "Well, he wasn't, well, not at first," she explained. When I returned to take care of my ailing father, here is where I ran into him. I avoided any interaction with him. I left him, and my family, without warning, but he tracked me down. He was familiar with your dad but not with you. When I informed him about you, I was planning to take you with me, but then your dad found out about him and insisted you remain with him. I was forced to do it.

My chest rose in a huff.

An option is always available, I told him. "That's not anything my father would have ever said. He would have defended you and us at any cost. For what possible reason would you choose a stranger over the person you've loved for years?

It's difficult to describe," she said. "When the time came, your father found out about my history, and he took it very personally. I never stopped thinking about you, Leah.

I looked at her blankly, trying to decide whether she was telling the truth about the final bit.
Her words, "Leah, I know that want to live with your buddy," made me sit up a little straighter in my chair. But the law requires you to dwell with a relative until you're eighteen, and since I'm the only relative you have left, I'd want to make things up to you. Even though I can never get back the time I lost with you, I would want to start again with you.

I gave her a blank look, but she persisted.

My mother came forward and put a hand just on the bed next to me. I backed away from her because I felt uncomfortable.

Her expression became melancholy as her gaze remained fixed on mine. I'm not here to dispute with anybody, but I would want to propose," she replied. You stay with me for an entire year, and then when you reach eighteen, you're free to go. I won't even beg you to remain if you don't ask me why. I'll let you go, but you have to hang around for an entire year.

My eyes were wide as I looked at her. After a year, she was ready to let me go.

Could I survive here for a year? Well, whatever this is.

She remarked to me, "All I want is for you to get up to know me," and that snapped me out of my reverie.

I could not take my eyes off her.
To paraphrase, "I won't force you into something you don't want. She gave him a blank stare and said, "I desire that you know I would just have waited until the end of the month. I know my appearance at your father's burial didn't make a

good impression, because Julian is a harsh head; he seldom thinks before he speaks. Even so, there was a crisis in our little town, which meant that I was informed that I had to assure you were okay.

My eyes landed on her. Where do we stand? I wondered, but I had a sneaking suspicion that even if I questioned her, she still wouldn't tell me.

I was silent, but I did give some attention to what she had said. My only choice was to remain here for a year, but I wasn't without options; I could always return home, and I could always wait till... but then my mind gave me a curveball in the form of an idea, and a plan began to take shape in my thoughts, something I could strive towards.

There was no way I could have stayed with her.

It was strange to consider the possibility of meeting my mother. My first 8 years of existence were spent close to her. If I'm being really honest, she is somebody I loved, but right now it was too complicated to care.

What was the appropriate response to all of this?

When someone you know up and departs without saying goodbye or giving a reason, it's only natural to feel resentful. What kind of human being she is today is unknown to me; she may be the same or she may be different, but I chose not to find out. I had Dani and Lucy back home who were more like family than she would ever be, so the idea of spending a year with her felt like a manipulative ploy. Everything she did, I realized, was for her benefit, not mine.

What if she hadn't gotten a call from the clinic? What if she hadn't bothered at all? Understanding my father's desire for me to contact her was

anything different; he had the winning formula for me. Even if he sat down next to me as I has spoken to her, he would just have waited for me to cool off and give my consent before moving on.

It wasn't my choice to remain here; in fact, she had been the one that abandoned me.

I relaxed by shutting my eyes and breathing deeply.

My head was beginning to ache once again.

When I finally managed to open my eyes, I focused.

How about if I decide I don't desire to get to meet you? I could only manage a mumble.

My mum looked at me strangely but said nothing.

So why should I bother? Indeed, I did enquire. You haven't spent any time spending time with me in the last nine years, yet now all of a sudden you want to start dating me.

I didn't let my mother finish her sentence. I had much to do.

I responded, "Did you ever consider that I had a life back home? I mean, okay, I completed school, but I additionally had my sports. Where do they stand? If only...

She called my name, "Leah," but I stared at her.

"What?" Indeed, I did enquire.
My brain ached even more, but I had to let her know what I was thinking.

At one point, I yell, "You believe that for me to remain with you, I must remain pleasant and an affectionate daughter to you. I didn't feel like coming here. It's not about me; I'm just trying to make you seem nice.

I didn't give a damn if my mother was trying not to weep.

I could no longer take her treatment of me.

Not with her, I wouldn't have to do any nonsense.

To make sure she can't see me, I flip over in bed and lean back. I'd had enough at that point.

I yell, "Just leave me alone!" I don't wish to have any contact with you.

The constant pounding in my brain forced me to shut my eyes.

She said, "Leah," but I stuffed my hands in my ear to muffle the sound.

I can't see staying with her. I would leave as frequently as I could, even if it meant leaving for a whole year.

I avoided her at all costs.

Eventually, I was able to shut my eyes.

As thoughts of escape were racing through my brain, I was starting to feel drowsy.

I hoped that the yellow eyes wouldn't be there as I closed my eyes because I needed sleep again.
I had my fingers over my ears, yet I still managed to hear something. I didn't feel like giving her another go at communicating with me.

My eyes remained closed as a heavy sensation washed over me, and then I led into the night where I encountered nothing.

When I realized it wasn't yellow eyes, I felt a sense of relief.

What the heck was I doing? Yet sleep overtook me; my eyelids became heavy, and I shut them, allowing the tranquility to carry me away, if only for a little.

Chapter 13

I couldn't disturb her as she slept in the dark.

I had to check our whereabouts.

I was sent to her by the moon deity.

I was supposed to go when my twelve birthday arrived, but the moonlight goddess informed me I had to wait until she was ready. After a long wait, the moon goddess granted me two wishes: a window into her life and the ability to cover my fragrance.

While I waited for the right moment to make my appearance, the goddess always said no. However, I kept getting the same response: I had to await.

I was able to see everything going on in the recesses of her mind.

After her mother abandoned her, leaving her in her father's care, I saw my human crumble into a shell of herself. She never fully healed, but she is a tough biscuit who knows how to care for herself.

I have seen this person rip apart her heart even though she believes her mother loved her. On the evening in question, she had a fight with her father overseeing my mother again and was hellbent on not going or anything else to salvage what was left with her mom. It occurred so quickly, yet I could feel what was about to

happen slowly; that night was never intended to be, and I had to get to the top. She was in danger, and even the goddess warned me to stay away.

Once she was knocked unconscious, I decided to make my move. Just as he murdered her father, the wolf would have killed her. As my eyes were open, he slashed her father's neck. When he saw me, he was amused since he had never imagined that she would have me. His eyes blazed yellow, but I saw her stirring, and I had to act swiftly to murder him before he could realize he was mistaken.

I traveled even further into the dark recesses of her mind and the distant past.

The moon goddess approved, but warned me to be cautious. There was even more to the wolf tale, but she wouldn't tell me since she doesn't meddle in her kids' affairs.

I couldn't tell her the truth about what I overheard.

I heard the whole conversation between the wolf and her father; he gave money, but not to the wolf.

I had to keep my human safe, and I always will.

I had to give in to the wolf's dreams; she needed to get some shut-eye. I bear the responsibility for her lack of sleep. I had to teleport her far back into her subconscious.

I had to reveal myself quickly.

Everyone will be surprised, I know, but it's for the best.

But because our partner is in this area, I must be present.
I had to talk to him.

That's why I had to be near him at the time.

The task of dealing with my human was not easy. She will prove to be a formidable opponent. I've met several of her ex-boyfriends, and they were vile. If I had been there, I definitely might have kicked their butts. I fantasized about slitting their necks whenever she was around.

My eyes widened as I took in my surroundings.

There was nobody there.

There was no evidence of her mother.

While I was aware of the depth of my human's resentment of her mother, I had never idea it could reach that level.

My human had a lot more pent-up anger against her because of the loss of her mother. She felt the urge to vent.

The realization that she was considering leaving the group was painful.

because I wanted this place but she had no idea who we were or that we had a mate in this area.

I felt his presence close by.

As I listened to the moon goddess and restrained myself, we discovered a way to hide odors from one another.

His perfume struck me deeply, and I can only imagine the sparks she would have felt had our scent not been masked. I was tempted to go forward and let them lay claim to us, but I reminded myself to relax.

My human needs to sleep, so I'll have to penetrate deeper into her head again.

I had to feel my human's pain as I considered all that had occurred to her over the years. There were good times, too, especially as they related to her relationship with the other human female she bothered to pursue.

I was moved by the human friend's and her mother's attempts to comfort and possibly adopt her in the wake of her father's death.

It broke my heart to see how things turned out. I listened as her mother, her mother's brother, and her mother's partner all claimed they were going to take her immediately.

I was quite incensed by them.

As a wolf, it is your responsibility to eliminate any dangers to you or your human, but I was not ready to come up for air just yet.

I felt terrible that I was giving her migraines. Being in the back of her mind was fine while she was little, but not so much when her human was a preteen. Don't even get me starting on teenagers and their hormones; their thoughts are all over the place.

As much as I wanted to go forward and stay with her, I knew I had to respect the moon goddess's wishes. We trusted her judgment because she was our mother.

Outside, I could make out some noise.

When I prepared to shut my eyes, I caught his aroma.

Our companion was waiting for us outdoors.
As I realized I wasn't supposed to advance just yet, my heart gave a little flutter of excitement before sinking again.

I was curious about his appearance and background.

In my mind, I was mulling over every scenario, but I was certain that I would see him shortly.

The aroma stimulated me, but I had no way of letting him know I had come.

With a deep sigh, I shut my eyes.

Back on the surface, I pushed his human but kept close by.

I was aware that, at least for the time being, I needed to keep my dream secret from her.

I followed her around but didn't go too near in case she had been a werewolf.

As soon as I heard it door open, I covered our fragrance.

His aroma was so strong that I had no doubt it was our match.

I was forced to head back, but as a powerful hand touched ours, something within me sparked. We are successfully forming a mating link, and he will sense it. He has no reason to think that we will too.

I had to shut my eyes and take a deep breath in.
His aroma was intolerable, but I was able to figure out who he was and I was astonished by what I saw.

His dominance was unquestioned.

One of us was the pack leader.

My emotions were higher, but as soon as her hand left mine, humans, I felt bereft.

Defeated, I let out a sigh.

I retreated to a more hidden part of my human psyche.

I told myself, "Leah, it won't be long." Your fortunes are about to improve significantly.

Back in the shadows, I stretched out and put my head in his paws.

The Moon Goddess assured me that she will show herself to me at the appropriate time.

Until she does, I must sit here in the shadows.

There was no way around it; I would just have to tell her exactly who and what were.

I hope someone does, since else things will become tricky for me.

My eyelids closed because I knew it was best to give my human some more slumber.

Chapter 14

Cassie created a mental connection and informed me that Leah was now conscious. My heart shattered while I was at work because she mentioned Leah.

When Lynx found out she was alive and insisted I come to visit her, she was relieved.

We headed to the clinic, but I overheard Jenny's whole chat with the receptionist as I walked in.

Her rage was palpable; she was upset with her mother.

I had to sneak a peek and listen. No child, werewolf or normal, should have to go through what Leah did when she was a kid.

As rage coursed through our veins, I sensed Lynx nodding his head in agreement.

Leah had my deepest sympathies. She was justified in her anger, but Jenny's behavior ensured a horrible outcome for both of us.

After what seemed like an eternity, the door suddenly opened, and Jenny, obviously unhappy, came out.

The nurse was staring at me, so I glanced at her. Her gaze was fixed on me the whole time.

"What's her status?" I cleared my voice and moved closer to her to inquire.

I couldn't risk entering while she was still awake. I'm a stranger to her.

The doctor's assistant cracked a grin.

She looked at the door of my mate's room and stated, "She's doing well, considering Alpha." "Her headaches are more of a cause for concern, and they appear to worsen under stress."

The nurse offered me a brief, kind grin as she examined me.

She added, somewhat reddened by the effort, "I believe her mother is pressing her too hard."

She turned her attention back to the door and apologized for her outspokenness, saying, "I heard all that was said and I believe her kid deserves an opportunity to get over everything." She's just lost her dad and is ready to uproot to a new city, and she has no idea what werewolves are.

She was correct in her assumption that she was ignorant of our race.

The nurse's eyes widened as I muttered, "I suspect the same." But her mom represents the only family that has left, and I think Leah needs some time to recover and heal from all that has happened.

The nurse scowled.

She claimed, "I suppose her friends volunteered to take her in," adding afterward that she wished she hadn't.

The lynx frowned.

"They did," I mused, cocking my head to examine Leah's front door. I peeped in and heard nothing but a gentle snoring. She had dozed off.

I smiled at the nurse and said, "I'll have to talk to Jenny."

That was acknowledged by the nurse.

I got up and went to Leah's door to leave.
When I finally got up the nerve to open the door, I saw that my roommate was fast sleeping.

I pushed the door gently shut after entering.

I made my way to the edge of the room and gaped at her.

Leah looked stunning, yet her hair was a mess since she was resting in a hospital bed.

As I grasped her hand, tingles shot through my body and caused me to sweat profusely. I examined her little hand next to mine.

Lynx made a sound like a whine and moved.

'Partner,' he referred to himself as.

I said, "I know."

For a while, I just stood there, but eventually, I had to go going. I didn't want her to recognize me since we were strangers.

I dropped her hand and walked away, heading for the exit. After my hand touched the doorknob, I turned around to see. I cast an anxious glance back over my shoulder.

What I needed was her help.

When I exited, I caught sight of the nurse who had been observing me from the nursing station.

I approached her with a grin on my face.

Let me know what's going on, I replied, adding, "Mind connecting me with anyone who has an issue; I know Jenny believes she knows best." Any little point."

The doctor or nurse nodded and grinned.
I got up and left the hospital room. I went to the packing house and then to the office. Even though my heart was sad, I smiled and welcomed everyone.

I know I need to inform the pack that I have discovered my mate, yet I'm unable to do so until I have established my identity and explained the situation to Leah.

When I arrived at work, Zain was already at my desk. He cast a grin over his shoulder.

He enquired, "How is she?"

Waking up, I walked over to our desk and greeted myself.

To which Zain gave a resounding yes.

When are you going to approach her, he enquired.

I frowned involuntarily.

The main issue seems to be that Jenny and Leah battled over the entire scenario of her moving in with her, but I responded, "Oh, maybe soon."

Zain looked at me intently, but he said nothing.

I stared at him and added, "I overheard some more of the talk." Jennifer is the person whom Leah despises the most.

She is also justified in her actions," he said bluntly. At the age of eight, she left her. As a youngster who adored her parents, they needed her.

He cocked his head as he met my gaze, and I gazed back.

He questioned, "Are you concerned there may be problems once she leaves?"

That got a yes from me.

I warned her that if Jenny didn't back down a little, she'd end up with no one to push back against. Leah needs time to think this over.

To which Zain gave a resounding yes.
He looked at me and remarked, "That's true." It must be an awful load for her to process, what with her father's recent death and the fact that she was relocated against her choice.

Defeated, I let out a sigh.

I added, "I have already recruited a nurse to let them know what's going on and any potential concerns with Jenny. We need to keep additional eyes on the situation."

Zain nodded, but his thoughts were elsewhere.

I'm curious as to your thoughts. Indeed, I did enquire.

Zain groaned and gave me the eye.

He added, "I was simply wondering if it might be better if she remained here, but since she doesn't learn anything about our type, would be a horrible decision to make."

My heart starts beating every time I consider Leah being here. That way, I could see her often.

As I turned to look at Zain, he gave me and knowing nod.

He then remarked, "You agree."

Reclining back my chair, I said, "I do; but, we will see what occurs since I have a weird feeling that I may have to intervene if things go out of sorts."

To which Zain gave a resounding yes.

Defeated, I let out a sigh.

What's the latest on the frontier? Indeed, I did enquire.

There were no rogues in sight when a guardian mentally linked them earlier to report that he had smelt them at the south side. On I went to meet Leah, I asked Zain to have a look.

Zain scowled at me as he gazed at me. He looked at me and remarked, "That's true." It must be an awful load for her to process, what with her father's recent death and the fact that she was relocated against her choice.

Defeated, I let out a sigh.

I added, "I have already recruited a nurse to let them know what's going on and any potential concerns with Jenny. We need to keep additional eyes on the situation."

Zain nodded, but his thoughts were elsewhere.

I'm curious as to your thoughts. Indeed, I did enquire.

Zain groaned and gave me the eye.

He added, "I was simply wondering if it might be better if she remained here, but since she doesn't learn anything about our type, would be a horrible decision to make."

My heart starts beating every time I consider Leah being here. That way, I could see her often.

As I turned to look at Zain, he gave me and knowing nod.

He then remarked, "You agree."

Reclining back my chair, I said, "I do; but, we will see what occurs since I have a weird feeling that I may have to intervene if things go out of sorts."

To which Zain gave a resounding yes.

Defeated, I let out a sigh.

What's the latest on the frontier? Indeed, I did enquire.

There were no rogues in sight when a guardian mentally linked them earlier to report that he had smelt them at the south side. On I went to meet Leah, I asked Zain to have a look.

Zain scowled at me as he gazed at me.
Zain sat back in his chair and remarked, "As the guard stated, there was a slight smell of rogues mostly on the south side, but there wasn't a way to determine if they were traveling by or scoping out the pack. Unfortunately, we must wait.

I scowled.

It sounded awful, and I couldn't stand it.

While thugs were never a major problem previously, a handful has stopped by in the past three months. Finding out whether they were excellent or terrible took some time.

I don't like lawbreakers, but if they're only passing through, I'll let them alone. I see no need to initiate anything unnecessary.

Defeated, I let out a sigh.

Zain replied, "I discovered some information regarding Leah," which caused me to give him a puzzled look.

As in, "What do you mean?" Indeed, I did enquire.

Zain snickered.

Hey, I did say you I would dig into her social media and see if I may discover anything about her," he remarked, getting out of his seat. He got to his feet and came nearer to my workstation.

Zain sifted through my desk's stack of papers, extracted a blue box, and gave it to me.

"Here," he proclaimed.

I looked through the file, fascinated by the pictures he had taken of her that were included.

I raised my eyes to meet his.

Zain got up, a grin on his face.

He stated, "I saw pictures of her from the high school she went to, and she's very into athletics and wants to stay in shape." There are plenty of pictures of her and her dad, and she has a lot of friends.

My gaze returned to the folder as I nodded.

As we went over a picture of her, I could sense Lynx draw near to look at it, and I heard a howl in my brain.

Zain pulled me away from him and murmured, "Carson," as our gazes locked. He cracked a smile.

I couldn't be happier for both you and Lynx, he told me.

Laughter lit up my face.

I'll keep everyone away from you so you can read what I discovered, he promised; then they could figure out when and how you'd meet her.

That got a yes from me.

Having the chance to finally meet Leah has sent waves of joy through me.

Lynx agreed & wanted to go back there, but she understood that we would have to wait.

I'm not sure how much longer I can hold out till we meet her.

Chapter 15

Feeling something beside me woke me up and caused me to open my eyes.

The nurse unhooking me from the cables caught my attention. As she looked into my eyes, she grinned.

"Can I get you anything?" she inquired.

I smiled and looked at her.

Despite only being awake for a short while, I was able to feel completely refreshed. Not once could I recall the golden eyes; maybe they had faded along with the dream.

I started to glance around the room when the nurse suddenly entered.

The expression on her face when she stated, "She's not here," made me blink twice.

"Your mom," she said, "She departed after you went back to sleep." But I believe she will return;

she needed to speak with the doctor and I expect to see him on his rounds very soon.

The two of us were staring at one other.

"When can I check out?" I felt anxiety at the prospect of going since I knew I used to have to remain with my mom, but I asked nonetheless.

The nurse gave me a blank look and a shrug.

Smiling, she continued, "The doctor will have to let you know" as she headed out the door. "I'll be seeing you soon."

I relaxed onto the bed with a grin on my face.

For the time being, my mind was clear, but if mom came back in here, who knows what might happen?

I had no idea what to do.
I had to get out of there and return home.

After a while, my mother came in and stared at me as I began to go over various options in my mind.

I scowled.

Her bloodshot eyes fixed on mine for a while. It was obvious that she had been upset.

My attention was riveted as my mother made her way to the chair and sat down. She then turned to me and said, "The doctor will be in..." she began, but the doctor entered the room, smiling, cutting her short.

He introduced himself to Leah by saying, "Nice to meet you finally."

I gave him a blank gaze and said nothing.

The doctor came in and positioned himself at my bed's foot. He picked up my charts from the foot of the bed, glanced them over briefly, and then turned to face me.

He looked over to my mom and said, "Well, we're going to be keeping you in again for the night in case you're well, but she may be good to leave tomorrow afternoon."

I gave him the cold shoulder and just looked.

What the heck are those two folks doing to make me feel like I'm not in the same room as them? And that's exactly what occurred just now.

Between the two of them, I cast my gaze.

So I responded, "I guess I can go tomorrow."

The doctor returned my gaze and nodded.

He answered, "Well, you'll then have to take a rest, and I advise resting for a few days for your expedition outdoors, but I'll schedule you for a checkup to see me. The headaches are something I need to monitor. If things don't look well when you go home, I'll send them for the next scan.

I gave him the cold shoulder and just looked.

Mom cracked a grin.
Okay, I'll see u tomorrow, Leah, he added.

Without uttering a word, I watched him make his way to the exit.

I focused on the entrance but felt my stomach tighten as my mother made a tiny adjustment.

I avoided her like the plague.

She mumbled, "Leah."

I shut my eyes tight and disregarded her.

I don't understand why she'd want to contact me again.

She understands how I feel, and it wouldn't have altered in the time that she was away.

She looked at me and said, "Please, Leah."

When I started, I made a face.

I sputtered and scowled, "I don't want to speak to you."

Ma sighed.

There was a period of uncomfortable quiet in the room. I kept my eyes moving, but never on my mother.

I had to get going right away.

A guy stepped into my room after a few moments when the door flung open.

I gave him the cold shoulder and just looked. I was familiar with him. He smiled at me but then walked towards my mom.

Where had I seen him before? Even more, thoughts were racing through my head as I saw him approach my mom and bend to kiss her on the cheek. He stepped back and put a supporting arm on the seat behind her.

He introduced himself with a simple "hi."

I was completely silent.

Really, who was he?

My mom shook her head.

She looked at me while then glanced at the guy and said, "Leah, this is Josh."

I just gazed at them.

Seeing him stare at her before returning his gaze to mine, I felt a sharp stab of pain.

The expression he gave her was one I'd recognized from long ago. My father still had the same expression for her as he had when they were married.

Josh's obvious feelings for her were obvious to me.

I gaped but didn't say anything at all.

Josh inquired, "How was your visit to the doctor?"
When is she going to get home?

My mother turned back to me and said, "She
should be home tomorrow afternoon."

I just didn't feel at home here.
What the heck was I meant to think at this point?

More than anything, I felt numb.

Josh swallowed a little air.

That's great news," he added with a grin. "We have
a room set up and waiting for you."

Wonderful acting like a perfectly happy family, are
we?

As I made my way toward the exit, I saw that both
Josh and my mom were staring at me.

Leah, I interrupted my mother as she started to say.

Looking back at her, I responded, "I don't want to
remain with you."

Her gaze never left me, but the uncomfortable silence had returned.

I had no idea how to behave around them.

As Josh called my name, I looked up at him. He let out a heavy sigh.

We just want to ensure you're alright after all you've gone through," he continued, eyeing my mom and me. "I realize this is all new. After you've unpacked and made yourself at home, we can talk about anything. There's more we can get into, but first, you and your mom need to..."

With renewed rage, I spat, "You don't know what my mom and I need."

I felt my head beginning to pound, and so I shut my eyes. After a few moments of heavy breathing, I finally cracked them open.

I turned around to see Josh and my mom watching me with worry on their faces.

I yell, "Would you just stop staring at me like that!" I had zero interest in what they had to offer.

Just as I was ready to lose it completely, the door was open, and a guy and a woman strolled in.
I just gazed at them.

Really, who are these individuals?

The lady resembled my mother when she was younger, and the man resembled the other man my mother had just dated. I could see that they were linked, but I couldn't figure out how. Who raised her?

As my gaze finally settled on the older guy, the tension in the room was too much for me to bear.

He stared right at me.

Stubbornness set in on his face. It was obvious he didn't care for me or want him around.

My mom finally spoke out after clearing her throat: "Dad, I told you please wait until I talked to her." Do not make your introductions at this moment.

Now at the foot o my bed stood an elderly couple, and I glanced at them.

Even though the lady was kind, it was the male who made the first impression. Even though he's her dad and my grandpa, he seemed just as eager to escape me as I was. As he looks at my mom, the disgusted expression fades away.

We were eager to meet her, he said.

My eyes were wide and my head was throbbing as I peered at him; this couldn't end well.

Again, I should have closed my eyes, but I kept looking about.

My grandfather's face stiffened as he glanced at me.
Nothing came out of my mouth.

My grandma approached from the side and remarked, "You must be Leah," which made me turn to look at her.

I scowled.

It was wonderful to meet you, she added as she extended her hand. I glanced up at her while still focusing on her hand.

I decided not to shake it.

There was no familiarity between us.

My mother only just informed me that she had a family, and before that I had no idea. She didn't talk about her family once while she was staying with us, not in front of either dad or myself.

My grandma withdrew her hand, wincing in pain.

The granddad gave out a really angry vibe as I glanced over at him.

Unease crept over me.

No one here was anybody I knew.

The devil knew why they were all here.

I glanced at my mother, who was wearing a peculiar face.

I shook my voice clean.

I fabricated my "I need sleep" excuse.

I need privacy at that time.

I stood there while everyone exchanged glances and eventually filed out of the room, leaving just my mother and myself.

My mother made her way towards the exit.
Let the fury out: "You know, it was wonderful being exposed to your girlfriend and family. If you wanted to play happy families, you could have waited until I got out of the hospital.

When my mother saw me, she stopped what she was doing and just looked at me.

When she said, "I know you are furious," I shrugged my shoulders.

I said, "I'm upset, fine." You've made it your goal to keep my life terrible, so I'm stuck here even though I don't want to be around you, this location, or those people. I will do my best to abide by your regulations, but a year from now just can't get here soon enough!

I saw the pain in my mother's eyes and wondered what would happen to me. That I would forget what she had done was beyond her wildest dreams.

Mom just left me there as she went out the door.

I focused my attention on the entrance but could hear a commotion outside. To be more accurate, they were shouting.

I groaned and stretched out on the bed.

I needed to leave here right now.

I wouldn't stick around and hope they warm up to me.

At night, there would be no one around, so I waited.

I considered sleeping for a bit; I'd need all my energy for the trip back.

Chapter 16

I was startled awake by a sudden tightening of something around my arm.

When I peered around the room, a nurse leaped back but immediately recovered.

"You're alright," she sighed.

She said, "No one's here," and I looked at her.

I just sat back and said nothing.

As I turned to the window, I saw that it was completely black outside.

Ok, good, I'm free to go.

The nurse continued to take my vitals while I observed. She finished up with a grin on her face.

There you have it, she said. There would be a closing time shortly, so please be patient if you need anything, however I may provide it to you immediately if you like.

My head trembled.

I said, "No, I don't need anything."

The doctor nodded and looked at me strangely.

"I apologize if this seems impolite," she prefaced. I overheard what happened earlier with your family and I must say that you handled it quite nicely.

A little grin crossed my face as I glanced at her.

The nurse cracked a grin and a sigh.
She finally remarked, "I will leave you to go back to sleep."

I agreed and nodded.

I observed as she gathered up her supplies and left the building.

There was a little delay as I waited.

When the shift changes, I'll be able to depart.

Now that somebody has seen me, no one will dare to come here.

Outside, I could make out the sounds of people talking and walking.

I glanced around to see if someone had left me any clothing, but there was nothing.

It seems that I am now lounging about the house in my hospital gown. I knew eyes would be on me, but I didn't mind. Please get me out of here as soon as possible.

I got out from under the covers and pulled them down to liberate my legs. My feet finally touched the floor as I sat up. I would have to take my time, but I figured that if I could get out of the hospital well before shift change, no one would even notice that I was missing.

As I tried to get out of bed without holding on to the side, my legs immediately felt like jelly and I had to sit back down.

Sighing, I finally gave up.

Poor body.

Please get to work for me.
I gave it another shot, this time being careful not to tumble backward before regaining my footing. Ahead, I took a deep breath and calmed myself.

One baby step at a time, I made my way to the entrance.

As I opened it to check if anybody was outside, I overheard two nurses having a conversation inside.

I sighed as I locked the door behind me.

I repositioned myself and rested my back against the wall.

I had to get away from here.

I glanced around and saw just a window, which obviously wouldn't allow me to escape. It seemed as if I were many stories high since my vantage point looked out over a forest.

There was a risk of falling if I made any sudden movements, such as jumping or lowering myself.

As I waited, I kept an eye on the entrance.

The nurses must have switched shifts.

After reversing course and entering the nurses' station, I found it deserted. I unlocked the door and peeked outside to make sure no one was there.

Not a soul in sight.

I let out a sigh of relief and left the room.

As I backed away, I rested my hand on the wall for stability.

I ducked low, hoping that nobody would catch me, but I couldn't help but wonder whether the lady in the backless medical gown would give me away.

As I rounded the corner at the foot of the stairs, I ran straight into a solid object.

As I tripped and fell, I landed hard on my behind.

I winced and turned to see what I had so forcefully impacted.

Being confronted with a leg forced me to examine my assailant carefully. As I got closer, I saw that the person in front of me had stunning chocolate-brown eyes, and I knew I was in for a treat.

Holy crap! He has good looks.

First, I didn't even know I was gazing at him until my pulse rate had skyrocketed.

His eyes were staring straight at me, and the corner of his lips quirked up.
My cheeks began to redden.

He said, licking his lips, "Are you done looking me out?"

More heat sprang in my cheeks.

Please don't take what I said the wrong way. I murmured, avoiding her gaze as I glanced elsewhere.

As I turned back around, the guy in front of me was on his knees. Let me assist you up, he said, extending his hands.

I put my hands in his, and electricity coursed through me.

My eyes landed on him. When he lifted me, his attention was fixed on me.

I attempted to get up and take a stride, but my legs had so many ideas, and I ran into him again. Luckily, he grabbed me this time.

Sorry, I whispered as I rested my head on his shoulder.

The man was nearby. As I put my arms on his broad shoulders, he lowered himself to pick me up and carry me like a bride. I felt like his scent was penetrating right into my being.

I can't help but gaze at him.

I got you, he whispered as he dragged me to my bedroom. That wasn't where I wanted to be, but being in its arms made everything okay.
Silently, I let the man carry me into my bedroom and set me down on my bed. After setting me down, he checked to make sure my legs were secure.

The guy straightened up and gave me an intense stare.

Carson, he referred to. Hi, I'm Carson.

My mouth became a grin.

Looking at the seat, I introduced myself as Leah. What's the matter, man?

Carson took the seat and didn't take his gaze off me as he sat down.

"So why were you trying to get away?" His inquiry was direct. Someone who is hospitalized must be sick.

I gave him the cold shoulder and just looked.

What was I planning on conveying to him when I told him I was ready to go?

I shook my voice clean.

When I was leaving, I expressed my want to go. Even if his eyes were beautiful, I decided it was best not to lie to someone who has offered assistance.

Oh no, I can't afford to look at him. There would be problems with him.
In my absence, he continued talking.

His question "Why?" caused me to turn around and stare at him.

With him, I immediately relaxed. I felt the want to fill him in on additional details because of him.

My dad grew up as an only child. He was an only child; his parents passed away within four years of one another. My father was the single person I ever had that I felt comfortable confiding in about anything, and now that he's gone, I have nobody.

Carson was reclining in his seat, so I turned to see him.

He finally responded, "You may as well tell me." I'm free from pending obligations.

I gaped, but eventually let out a sigh.

My mother, I told her. I have to move in along with their new family because she is making me.

Carson agreed.

He probed, "You don't like them, do you?"

I scowled.

I said, "Don't like them." I just met my mom's boyfriend/husband tonight, and now she needs me to play beautiful children with strangers.
My eyes landed on him.

I told him, "I met him today, along with my grandparents." "Are strangers to me? My dad and I used to be a pair, but now we're just me.

When he listens to me, Carson's expression relaxes.

I flat-out refused to become roommates with them. I didn't grow up with my mother in that way. She abandoned me when I was just 8 years old, and she has just recently returned to my life upon learning of my father's passing via a doctor. After a long time apart, she has found me and wants to play "happy families." I'm not capable of carrying it out.

The weight of my thoughts had returned, and they were tiring me out.

Carson looked at him with wide eyes.

He finally cracked it: "What will she do to what makes you happy?" I'm sorry for the loss of your father and I know you've gone through a lot.

I gave him the cold shoulder and just looked.

The only person who has apologized to me sincerely is a total stranger named Carson.

Leaning back in bed, I tucked the blankets about me.

I told my mom that she couldn't make me happy and that she should let me slowly warm up to new experiences and people instead of forcing me to accept them all at once. I just can't take it. My grandfather, in particular, gave me the impression that he intended to murder me every time he looked at me.
Carson stiffened ever-so-slightly and furrowed his brow.

Sighing, I finally gave up.

I expressed my desire to "return home" by saying as much. Everyone cared about me and wanted to take care of me. Not my mom, but me: we want them. I realized I could survive without her.

Carson cleared his throat and peered.

He muttered, "Don't leave," and I gave him a strange look.

Why would someone say such a thing?

Carson's stare became more intense, yet despite this, I felt calm and maybe a little more exhausted than I should have.

After a long day, Carson sighed.

He suggested I wait until I was "one hundred percent" before trying to make a "clean escape," adding, "Why don't you see what happens?"

Carson returned my grin with his own.

What I'm getting at, he walked near me and said. His hand is on the verge of touching mine. Go ahead and give it a go; if it doesn't work out, you could meet a person you'll trust who will assist you or perhaps take you in.

My breathing quickened as I fixed my gaze on him. With the expectation that he would turn out to be that guy.

Why was I behaving like a completely insane woman?

I've only just encountered him, but he has the most amazing chocolate eyes.

I gave my mind a mental shake and let out a sigh of relief.

I lied a little and replied, "I'll have to think about it." "My mom doesn't understand that I need space to go through things."

Carson agreed and cracked a grin.

You need to get some sleep," he stated as he got up to go.

"Are you able to remain?" I suddenly speak out, drawing his attention.

I swallowed hard, trying to remember why I'd just said that.

My genitalia were aching like hell.

How could I possibly harm him?

Ah! Quite, Leah!

Carson reseated himself in the chair.

Just till I go to sleep, I said softly as I faced him.

Carson agreed.

For the very first time in days, I felt a modicum of safety as I glanced at him.

It was the very first time since the accident that I felt safe, and I don't know what was going on, but Carson kept me feeling that way.

Shortly afterward, I felt my eyelids flicker and was plunged into total blackness.

As those bright eyes looked back at me, I realized I had been dreaming.

Oh no, not again!

Chapter 17

When my partner slept off, I observed.

What I had just heard made no sense at all.

Lynx was nearby and seemed to approve of our proximity to our partner. He felt entitled to her. When she spoke, he remained silent. As we took her up and carried her back to her room, he immediately calmed down.

The station nurse had mind link me to let me know that Jen and her family had got to the hospital to meet Leah, and I know it wouldn't go well.

This was not healthy for Leah, so I wanted to talk to Jenny about it. She couldn't take it any longer and attempted to flee the hospital.

As the door opened, I saw the nurse who had been there previously.

The leader apologized, "I'm sorry, alpha; I didn't realize you were in here."

I acknowledged her with a nod and turned back to Leah. On the bed, she seemed petite.

The nurse crossed to the opposite side to take her temperature and pulse. Her gaze was so close that I couldn't help but meet it.

She stammered out an apology.

I just responded, "If you have anything to say." "Say it."

The nurse gave me a pitiful look and sighed. Before she spoke, she stared at me intently.

That was a rough day for her, she said. Every single one of us nurses was shaken up by what we saw and heard.
I locked eyes with her, wanting her to keep talking.

That's strange. I said. You said that she had guests, but you didn't go into detail about what transpired.

The nurse glanced at Leah before returning her gaze to me.

What she said next, though, struck me by surprise: "Alpha, her mother presented her partner."

I raised an eyebrow when she remarked, "Then her grandparents arrived."

Jenny would certainly introduce Josh, but I was confused as to why her parents would be there. Her father stated explicitly that he had no interest in spending time with his daughter.

As in, "What the heck just happened?" After observing that the nurse is staring at me, I finally inquired.

She let out a heavy sigh.

She replied, "As usual, it concluded with your partner instructing them to go, but the trouble began when they did." As a group, they argued with one another. Her father wouldn't let her mother speak since "your partner wasn't part of the family," and her grandparents weren't invited.

I fixed my eyes on her, but a growl escaped my mouth that made the nurse jump.

I said, "I'm sorry." No disrespect intended against you.

The nurse nodded her head slightly.

This could never happen again, so I had to talk to Jenny and her family.

The fact that Leah was my mate was kept secret from all but a select few, yet anything was amiss, and I was forced to fix it or risk losing my mate forever.

I already know where to direct it if that day comes, and the rest of the pack will be forced to retreat in shame until they can convince her to come back. When Leah sprang up, my gaze shifted toward her.

The two of us were staring at one other.

I mean, what the heck was that?

I turned to see the nurse staring at her.

"Is this the first time she's tried that?" I inquired.

The nurse gave me a blank look and a shrug.

When she continued to examine her, she murmured, "She appears to be dreaming, alpha."

Staying here till she woke up would be odd, but I wanted to watch her sleep. Having just met her, I thought it was only fair to act kindly.

Lynx let out a disapproving grunt.

He moaned, "Why?" We can have her and ask her whatever we want to. Please don't send her to live with them; I forbid it. I don't have faith in them.

I gave him a return glance.

That's how I felt too. Jenny has been trying to force her to take on everything, and I felt like I had to speak up for her as her partner.

Lynx perked up in my mind.

We should call a meeting and lay out our demands without giving them any time to respond, he mumbled.

Lynx was correct in her assessment that we should contact her relatives.

First, I connected my thoughts with Zains.
"Are you there?" I inquired.

He murmured, "Good evening to you," as he prepared to leave the workplace and go home. Why? What are you doing?

I said, "I'm in the hospital; I had to take my wife back into her room when I found her trying to escape."

He looked at Lynx and said, "I defeated Lynx, and you enjoyed that." He knew his foolish face was grinning.

I cautioned, "Zain.

"I'm simply glad that you ended up meeting her," he apologized, "and I thought you gave her your name."

Yes, I answered. But that's not why I telepathically bonded with you in the first place.

That's OK, he agreed. So when you have some spare time, I would like all the specifics, but what do we want?

Sighing, I finally gave up.

I asked you to "please remain in the office" because of an urgent matter. I'm going to propose to Jenny in front of her whole family, and I need everyone to be a part of it.

Somewhat befuddled, he responded, "Alright, but why?" I'm the Beta; I have no business being there.

My response was, "I know, but I want you to see what I speak because if they don't follow what I'm about to recommend, I will put them on home arrest or, worse still, expel them."

What? he exclaimed. As in, "Why would you send them away?"

"I'm going to inform them what's going to happen when Leah gets home," I promised. "I found out that she had to deal with Josh coming to see her, which frightened her out. If my partner ever quits our pack, I will hold every member of this pack accountable.
Zain was silent for a moment before he sighed.

That's reasonable, he agreed. Worst case scenario: she does leave. After that, what are your plans?

After we'd had a chance to speak to them, I told him, "I need you there not only as a buddy but also as the Beta of the group. Please assist me with this.

"Yeah, dude," he said. Whichever path you choose, know that you have my support.

My mouth became a grin.

I told her, "I'll be there shortly." I'll send Jenny a mental connection to call her into the office.

Yeah, he replied.

I sighed and severed the mental connection.

Looking around, I noticed that the nurse, Leah, wasn't there; she must have left while I was head of Zain.

The second mental connection I made was with Jenny.

I told Jenny, "Josh, you and your parents need to come to my work in the next hour.

She began, "Alpha Carson, we just..." but I interrupted her with a snarl. In either an hour or I'll have to physically force everyone there.

With a sigh, I severed the mental connection.

It wasn't for myself, but for Leah, that I took action.

Given that I was her spouse, it fell to me to ensure her safety.

I glanced across at Leah and got out of my seat.

Tingles were running through me as I kissed her head, but I had to pull away and gaze at her from below.

I started to leave her room but turned around when I recognized the nurse who had just come in.

"Are you able to accompany her?" I inquired. Be on the lookout for her. I can't afford the distraction of worrying that she could try to flee again while I try to get this problem solved.

After her first shock, the nurse nodded swiftly.

When she left the nurse's station, she said, "Sure," and entered Leah's room.

My only thought as I walked past the hospital and towards the pack home was to make sure nobody there had any illusions about the consequences of trying to force my mate to leave.

Chapter 18

It was peaceful on the way back toward the pack home. The majority of the flock was probably at home or sleeping.

I went inside the packing house and saw Zain waiting in the office. He saw me walking in and gave me a grin.

I nodded and went to sit down at my desk.

Zain groaned and gave me the eye.

Someone who is "on a mission," he mumbled. "I recognize that expression, and I beg you not to murder anybody."

I rolled my eyes in his direction.

I imagined Lynx laughing at me, but I paid him no mind.

If they haven't arrived in an hour, I murmured, "you're going to get them."

Zain's eyes widened as he glanced at me.

He seemed astonished, but he added, "You are taking responsibility for this problem."

After a moment, I nodded.
Someone has to, I said. We are married. This is something I have to do. I'd rather her stay than go.

Zaid agreed.

For the last hour, I've been filling Zain in on my plans. Zain and Lynx both agreed with all I said.

He then said, "You want me to arrange a room where she can stay off your floor if this all blows to crap with her family, right?"

After a moment, I nodded.

"I don't want anybody except me and you around her," I told her. "It's important that my family learns to take my advice."

Zain nodded to prepare for his remark when the doorbell rang.

As Zain got up to answer the door, we exchanged glances.

A larger opening in the entrance allowed Jenny, his parents, and Josh to enter. They entered and stood before me in a line.

Once Zain closed the door, he stepped away and walked over to me. As a result, I enlisted his support by having him accompany me.

I jumped in with, "I'm going to go right to the issue," cutting off any more discussion. A nurse informed me through mind link that you four caused a commotion outside of Leah's room earlier.
Jenny said, "Alpha," but I silenced her with a snarl.

I said, "DO NOT DISTURB ME!"

Jenny jumped back, and the others followed suit.

Jenny looked at the parents and thereafter back at me as I stated, "I am going to hold this problem with Leah in my hands." Josh remained nothing.

I made a solitary proclamation: "I will say this just once. If you make a mistake, I'm moving Leah into the pack house.

Jenny's father yelled, "YOU CANNOT DO THAT!"

I let out a low roar.

Lynx came closer, clearly prepared to face anyone who dared to treat us badly.

I sprang up from my seat and shot the guy a glare, shouting, "I'M THE ALPHA." I, not you, will have the last say.

The guy gave me the evil eye.

Intending to remark, "If your father had been here, he would..." Zain interrupted him with a snarl.

I moaned, "My father's not here," and Zain touched my arm to get my attention. He was quite angry.

"ENOUGH PAUL," he said. If you have another outburst, you'll be spending the night in jail.

Paul gave him a stern stare, but his features hardened. When Jenny's mum reached for him to comfort him, I saw as he resisted and withdrew his arm away.

Jenny, who had been staring at her dad, turned around to look at me.

You want what's best for Leah, therefore I know you want her to move in together with you. That's OK, but I recommend keeping the home occupied by just you and Josh. Your parents can keep the kids until she's ready, whether they're with you or someone else, but they won't go on until I give the go-ahead.

Jenny turned to me, her expression blank.

I had to let her know that Leah had attempted to flee.

To which she replied, "Jenny," I said. "God only knows what might have happened to Leah if I hadn't gone to the hospital once I did."

Jenny's eyes widened in shock.

The words "she attempted to flee" escaped her lips, a hint of pain.

When I saw Josh put an arm over her, trying to reassure her, I nodded.

I reassured her that I had returned her to her bed and that she was safe in bed with a nurse looking over her. While approaching her, I believe you should be more cautious. Leah has expressed a desire for privacy, but her wishes have gone unheeded.

Jenny just looked at me blankly.

She then inquired, "Did she talk to you?"

After a moment, I nodded.

Jenny gave me a sad gaze before sighing.

Carson, Alpha," she proclaimed. "She's my kid; I really ought to..." I put out a hand to silence her and she froze. Don't, I pleaded with you. While she is your daughter, she cannot be expected to accept your absence from her life during the last several years. You and Leah must speak, but you must wait for her convenience. She can't be hurried or coerced.

A tear trickled down Jenny's cheek, altering the expression on her face somewhat.

I made it clear that I would not try to interfere. But I will protect and advocate for Leah as much as possible. I think it would be best if you and Josh made plans for the boys, but then the 3 of you went home tomorrow when Leah was ready to come back.

Jenny stared, but Josh only nodded.

We don't understand why our leader would be considering such a monstrosity. Paul's mutterings prompted a groan from Zain and me. I was becoming irritated by this guy.

Infuriating Paul more, I told Zain to lock him up for the night.

Zain made room and approached Paul, putting his arm over his shoulder and leading him through the door. Without a word, Paul looked at the hue of his wolf and then back to himself. As a result, he became irritated.

Not that it made any difference to me. I couldn't take the way he kept bringing up Leah. What possessed him to do that? Indeed, she was his grandchild.

Lynx barked and sounded eager to go. I think I succeeded in calming him down.

Once Zain and Paul had departed, I peeked in between the remaining people.

If Leah becomes unhappy or attempts to run and hide again, I will remove her from her care and place her in mine, I told her. Is that right?

Both Jenny and Josh nodded, and her mother just looked at me.

What am I meant to do?" she questioned. You locked up my partner and left me here all alone.

I gave a casual shoulder shrug.

That's none of my business, so I told him to go find a new roommate or risk getting kicked out myself.

Her mother gave me a startled look.

She said, "What does it mean?"

"Well, if either of you causes any trouble," I warned, "I will put you either in shutdown or a cell and will start coming up with only a punishment suited for you, might even suggest banishment."

I was oblivious to the screams of horror around me.

Her mother yelled, "You can't banish us!" She's just like us, you know. Why should she be treated like a queen while the rest of us are just pack members?

Despite sensing Lynx draw nearer, I shut my eyes. "Don't," I murmured, "Calm down."

Lynx hissed and backed away. He felt anxious.

After this, I may require a run.

As I widened my eyes and glanced at them again, I was met with worried stares.

"I will express this," I growled out. I can't stand it when people act like they're better than me. What I say is final since I am the pack's leader.

The three agreed with a nod.

"Now, I advise you leave," I whispered, "And think carefully what I have told."

Jenny and her mum nodded, turned, and left as Josh stared at me from the doorway.

"Your father would be pleased," he moaned. I understand your motivations. I should clarify that Jenny intended to introduce just me, and not them. They ignored her and crossed the line, but then when Jenny came up, Paul yelled at her about how rude Leah had been.

I looked at him blankly as he went on.

He said, "Jenny is your mate, and she wants the best for Leah, but she doesn't know about our type. Leah may find it challenging to adhere to the restrictions that Jenny and I have established since she is used to doing as she pleases.

I let out a low roar.

I clenched my teeth and said, "Josh, she's my mate, but I mean what I said; I'll take her away you Jenny, and your care."

Josh groaned and gave me the eye.

I get it," he replied, walking away.

When Josh stepped out, the door opened and Zain came in.

Zain sighed as he slammed the door behind him. "What was the deal with Paul?" he inquired. I've never even seen him so angry towards a member of the family before.

Defeated, I let out a sigh.

With a "I know" I responded. "Are you able to investigate him in any way?"

Zaid agreed.

Would be delighted to, he said. There's something wrong with him.

I got up from my seat without saying a word.

Zaion gave me a frowning expression in his eyes.

He inquired, "Where are you going?" as I left my desk.

I said, "I'm letting Lynx out," and in my mind, I heard Lynx flee, which startled me. I had to talk some sense into him many times in here. If he doesn't get the run he'll keep me up all night.

Zaid agreed.

May I join you? he enquired.

After a moment, I nodded.

Even though I knew Zain wouldn't respond, I couldn't have predicted how upset he would be over what occurred in the office just now.

The prescription called for a good run.

We left the office and walked around the entrance to the warehouse.

I gave Lynx free rein, and when he tore my clothing to shreds and jumped from the bottom of the group house stairs, he and Zain's wolf, Kai, took off sprinting.

Chapter 19

When I heard our partner go, I pulled Leah away.

I had to let her sleep through the nightmare since she was exhausted.

I knew a nurse was on hand, but knowing he was making an effort to keep us safe was reassuring, particularly after the family had paid their respects.

The identity of the elderly guy who made me nervous is unknown.

The moon goddess preferred that I remain hidden, but I had a human to safeguard. Our partner may do the same thing, but there was something about him that made me want to come out of hiding and show that my human is one of them.

Instead of helping him, it would have helped Leah. The situation seems to be getting worse and worse.

Now, more than ever, I had to keep my human safe.

While I am unable to open my eyes, I do recall that whomever our friend had hired to watch over us soon exited the room.

I got up as quickly as the door had closed.
I took a deep breath and found that his aroma continued to exist; it soothed me.

A sense of calm settled over me.

I took a glance around and realized Leah wanted to go. I couldn't stop her, however what were the odds that our mate would find her and bring her back to her hotel room?

I felt like I was on a cloud. The sound of his words and the smell of him made me want more of him.

The tingles were throughout my body.

It will be like an electric charge to her right now, but when I finally expose who I am, she'll be desperate for explanations and experience the tingles even more intensely. I'll tell her whatever she wants to know, even if it's about Carson, but first I have to make sure she's safe.

I lay back on the bed and beg the moon goddess for permission to defend my human right away.

There was an odd vibe in the air, and I felt obligated to be present for Leah no matter who or what was speaking to her.

I couldn't help but find it amusing.

Knowing how Leah has been acting recently, it's hardly surprising that she would fear she's going insane upon hearing the wolves howling for the first time.

I didn't want to frighten my human, however I did want to be at her side.

Another goal was to satisfy my yearning for my mate, but I anticipate that this will take more time than I anticipated since I know I will have to explain our culture and way of life to her.

I waited to see if anybody would show up, but nobody did.

Defeated, I let out a sigh.

Even though I knew That should relax, every moment of alone brought me back to the events of the previous evening. I wanted to murder the individual responsible, but I had no idea who he was. Leah and her father never knew him.

When my eyes begin to sleep, I give in to the exhaustion.

Knowing our luck, someone would stroll in and see the difference while I was trying to hide the fact that I was there.

I help Leah to the surface when her eyes shut so that she may take charge.

I shifted to the recesses of her memory.

After resting my head between my paws, I saw a dim light and got to my feet to investigate. That was the one I was expecting, and her arrival was met with anticipation.

My mother has been saying, "Tala," which means "I know users have been impatiently waiting to show yourself to our kid," for quite some time now.

Just thinking about it made me happy.

She went on, "I know I've been vague about why I held you back." After seeing what I saw, I don't think our kid is secure with the individuals assigned to care for her when she returns home.

Now that everything is coming to a head, I need your assistance in directing her.

I nodded at the goddess of the moon.

Tala, my kid, greeted him. You can show up in four days, but you won't be able to make any changes right away since I need u to wait.

That caused a frown on my face.

Why, I wondered.

She said, "Tala, so eager to turn into a wolf." That can't happen among the pack, but you will. When the time is right, she'll let you know.

"Where is our partner?" I inquired. Does he plan on assisting us?

The moon goddess never yelled, but she did speak quietly.

Sure, she answered. He will be her true mate, and he has already proved himself to be, but he must be patient until she realizes it.
I kept staring at the light because I was curious.

What are you not letting me in on? I inquired, prepared for the possibility that the lunar goddess would not answer.

No one spoke to me.

Defeated, I let out a sigh.

That's something I'll have to find out on my own.

My mother murmured, "You are one pushy wolf," and I cocked my head to the side, seeking to see whether she was kidding.

Nevertheless, I detected a shift in her tone, and she quickly added, "I didn't mean anything by it." Everything is always subject to shifts when it comes to a situation like these, but "Leah will just be thrown almost entirely to the wolves shortly," the source said.

I agree.

In a few days, you will show yourself to Leah, she added. "Keep covering your fragrance, but explain this to her so that you may both grow from the experience."

Is this any kind of lesson? I inquired.

The moon deity was amused.

She answered, "You may assume that." No wolf should have been acting the way you are, and I know that have been quite patient during this whole ordeal. I appreciate all you've done, including hanging out with the bad guy that one time.
I kept my mouth shut.

When the sunset, she said, "The rogue isn't the only person behind all this." Even while there are other factors at play, "having your voice among the pack helps lead her to become who they need to be," and "coming soon, more rapidly" will be possible thanks to the two of you working together.

I signaled approval with my head nod.

She promised, "I shall never leave you." "My dear, I look forward to our next meeting."

As soon as she finished speaking, the light went out.

In the shadows, I watched, yet I was content.

Not much longer now.

While I cannot show Leah my true shape, I can show her who I am.

A part of me wondered why we needed to break away from the rest of the group to accomplish it. It seemed inevitable that someone would try to harm Leah, what with all that was going on in the area, but who would assault a helpless human being?

When exhaustion takes hold, I rest my head on the front paws and close my eyes.

It won't be long now, Leah, and when it does come, you can count on me to be there to defend you.

When my eyelids drifted shut, I let out a yawn.

I wanted to get plenty of sleep before it was time to finally introduce myself to her.

As I finally got near, I had no idea what would happen, but I had to be ready for anything.

To keep my human safe, I had to do this.

The End

www.ingramcontent.com/pod-product-compliance
Lightning Source LLC
Chambersburg PA
CBHW070532220526
45467CB00003B/936